Volume XI, Number 10

Significant Issues Series

The Supreme Soviet: A Biographical Directory

by Dawn Mann, Robert Monyak, and Elizabeth Teague

foreword by Bill Bradley

Radio Free Europe/Radio Liberty
Munich

The Center for Strategic and International Studies, Washington, D.C.

Library of Congress Cataloging-in-Publication Data

Mann, Dawn.
    The Supreme Soviet: a biographical directory / by Dawn Mann,
Robert Monyak, and Elizabeth Teague: foreword by Bill Bradley.
    (Significant issues series, ISSN 0736-7136 : v. 11. no. 10)
    ISBN 0-89206-147-2
    1. Soviet Union. Verkhovnyi Sovet—Biography—Dictionaries.
2. Legislators—Soviet Union—Biography—Dictionaries. I. Monyak,
Robert. II. Teague, Elizabeth. III. Center for Strategic and Interna-
tional Studies. IV. RFE/RL, inc. V. Title. VI. Series.
JN6551.M36 1989   328.47'092'2—dc20
[B]   89-25198
                                                          CIP

The mission of the **Center for Strategic and International Studies**, founded in 1962, is to advance the understanding of emerging world issues in the areas of international security, politics, and economics. It does so by providing a strategic perspective to decision makers that is integrative in nature, comprehensive in scope, anticipatory in its timing, and bipartisan in its approach. The Center's commitment is to serve the common interests and values of the United States, its allies, and other friends.

Radio Free Europe/Radio Liberty (RFE/RL) is a private U.S. corporation funded by the U.S. Congress through the Board for International Broadcasting, an independent federal agency. RFE/RL is the leading broadcaster to Eastern Europe and the Soviet Union, on the air more than 1,000 hours per week in 23 languages. RFE/RL is also the principal nongovernmental center in the West for research on Eastern Europe and the Soviet Union. Its research, analysis, and news features, in addition to serving RFE/RL's own programming needs, are distributed widely outside the Radios—to government agencies and diplomatic missions, academic specialists and libraries, businesses, the media, and private citizens.

Contents

About the Authors

Dawn Mann is an analyst of Soviet internal politics with Radio Liberty in Munich. She is studying for her Ph.D. in political science at Georgetown University. She graduated Phi Beta Kappa with a B.S. in Russian area studies from the California State University at San Diego in 1984 and received her M.A. in Russian area studies from Georgetown University in 1987. She was a summer intern at Radio Liberty in 1986. She is the author of *Paradoxes of Soviet Reform: The Nineteenth Communist Party Conference* (Washington D.C.: Center for Strategic and International Studies/Significant Issues Series, 1988) and a frequent contributor to Radio Liberty's weekly *Report on the USSR.*

Robert Monyak is studying for his Ph.D. in political science at the W. Averell Harriman Institute for Advanced Study of the Soviet Union, Columbia University. He graduated Phi Beta Kappa with a B.A. in political science from Duke University in 1986 and completed an M.A. in political science at Columbia University in 1989. He worked as a summer intern at Radio Liberty in 1989.

Elizabeth Teague is an analyst of Soviet internal politics with Radio Liberty in Munich. She graduated from the University of Surrey in 1977, spent a year as a British Council exchange student in Voronezh, USSR, and received her doctorate from the University of Birmingham in 1986. In 1980 she was a summer intern at Radio Liberty. A frequent contributor to Radio Liberty's weekly *Report on the USSR,* she is the author of *Solidarity and the Soviet Worker* (London: Croom Helm, 1988) and coauthor of *Poezdka v SSSR* [*Trip to the USSR*] (London and Harlow: Longman, 1974.) She also contributed the chapter "Gorbachev's 'Human Factor' Policies" to the U.S. Congress Joint Economic Committee's compendium, *Gorbachev's Economic Plans* (Washington, D.C.: U.S. Congress, 1987).

Foreword

The election of the USSR Congress of People's Deputies and the recon-
stitution of the Supreme Soviet represent a potential turning point in the
democratization of the Soviet Union. The Supreme Soviet has not yet
become either a representative or a democratic body, but for the first
time in Soviet history the potential is evident.

Yet, all over the Soviet Union the winds of change are blowing.
The pace, even the direction, of that change is far from fixed. There
will doubtless be setbacks and turmoil. The skill of the new leadership
is bound to be severely tested. From time to time, the reformers may
lose their nerve or their way. *Perestroika* may get bogged down in
bureaucratic battles. The people's patience will be sorely tried.
Embattled Party bosses are struggling for their political lives. Some are
winning, others losing. But the people are tasting democracy. And they
want more. How do I know?

I met some of these newly elected deputies. They were insatiably
curious about the nuts and bolts of how a democratic congress actually
works. We talked for hours about the U.S. Congress. What its powers
and responsibilities are. The legal and institutional underpinnings of its
authority, like immunity and subpoena power. How the American
people measure Congress' openness and accountability. How it keeps
its independence from the executive branch. They shared their concerns
and their hopes.

The first election was far from perfect. In the final analysis,
2,895 candidates competed for 1,500 seats in the 2,250 seat assembly.
In 953 cases, two candidates ran for the same seat. In 384 cases in the
March election, one candidate ran uncontested. In 27 cases, four
candidates ran for the same seat. And in 14 cases, six or more candidates competed. Soviet voters had to cross out all the names on the
ballot that they did not want until one name was left. Where there was
only one candidate, a voter could cross his or her name out too—as a
vote against. Among those rejected were a number of high-ranking
Party officials and antireformers—to their and their Party's surprise and
embarrassment. We have reason to hope the next election will be more
open, perhaps with direct election to the Supreme Soviet.

Since the Supreme Soviet has met, it has become clear that they want to act like a Western legislature. They are moving to exercise the "power of the purse," the right of subpoena, etc. Those who are members of this unique body are listed and described in this volume prepared at Radio Liberty. The authors deserve considerable praise for their industry and insights. Western students of the Soviet Union will find this directory an invaluable reference.

Bill Bradley
United States Senator
September 1989

Preface

This directory, the only one of its kind anywhere (for now even in the Soviet Union), is the product of a fruitful collaboration between Radio Liberty (RL) in Munich and the Center for Strategic and International Studies (CSIS) in Washington, D.C.

It is hardly the first cooperative venture between these institutions. RL also makes an exceptional contribution to SOVSET'—the worldwide computer network on Soviet affairs operated by CSIS. Every one of the network's almost 500 members has daily access to a unique selection of analyses prepared by the Radio's fine research staff. The Center is pleased with its special relationship with Radio Liberty, which allows the latest information and most sophisticated interpretations to be distributed electronically.

It is a revealing measure of change in the Soviet system that a directory of the members of the Supreme Soviet could at last be thought useful. Our hope is that this volume will commend itself not only to scholars monitoring the parliament but to all those whose professional interests require that they begin to understand its workings—diplomats, businessmen, and many others.

A journalist covering a floor debate on, say, the "conversion" of tank plants to civilian uses will want to know which speakers on the subject have made their careers in military industry. An organizer of international exchanges among young parliamentarians will want to know whether the Supreme Soviet includes a significant contingent of members under 35 and whether their biographies in any way parallel those of the politicians he proposes to escort to the Soviet Union. A trade unionist trying to assess the political repercussions of the Donbass coal strike will want to know the background of those deputies who flew from Moscow to the coal fields to assume a mediating role between miners and managers. We should perhaps not completely exclude the idea that the directory will even have some usefulness to the members of the Supreme Soviet themselves.

In the rapidly moving politics of the Gorbachev era, you can't tell the players without a scorecard. CSIS and Radio Liberty are proud to be able to provide one. The pace of change, of course, also guarantees that it will soon be necessary to supplement the information provided here.

We urge readers of the directory to communicate with us and Radio Liberty about their experience with it and about improvements that would make subsequent editions even more useful.

Stephen Sestanovich
Director of Soviet and East European Studies
The Center for Strategic and International Studies

Acknowledgments

The authors are grateful for substantive help and advice to their colleagues, including freelance analysts and summer interns, at Radio Liberty and Radio Free Europe. We thank specifically Ferit Agi, Bess Brown, Dzintra Bungs, Elizabeth Carlson, Stephen Foye, Saulius Girnius, Gavin Helf, Toomas Ilves, Herwig Kraus, Vladimir Kusin, David Marples, Mirza Michaeli, Kathleen Mihalisko, Vello Pettai, Alexander Rahr, Ann Sheehy, Thomas Sherlock, Vladimir Socor, Julia Wishnevsky, and Victor Yasmann. We would also like to thank Patricia Early, Gertrude Kolarik, and Natalie Zuber of RL, who typed the list of deputies. Finally, the painstaking editing and formatting work done by Charles Trumbull of RL has been of immense value.

Munich

Abbreviations and Foreign Words

APN—Novosti Press Agency
ASSR—Autonomous Soviet Socialist Republic
AUCCTU—All-Union Central Council of Trade Unions
Autonomous okrug—administrative subdivision of a krai or oblast
CAC—Central Auditing Commission
CC—CPSU Central Committee
CP—Communist Party
CPD—Congress of People's Deputies
CPSU—Communist Party of the Soviet Union
DOSAAF—Voluntary Society for Cooperation with the Army, Air Force, and Navy
(F)—female
Gorkom—city Party committee
Ispolkom—executive committee of a soviet (local government body)
KGB—Committee for State Security
Komsomol—Young Communist League
Krai—administrative region; typically larger in area and less populous—but the administrative equivalent of—an oblast
Kraiispolkom—krai executive committee; see "ispolkom"
Kraikom—krai Party committee
MDG—Interregional Group of Deputies (independent group of CPD deputies founded in July 1989)
NKAO—Nagorno-Karabakh Autonomous Oblast
NTO—national-territoral okrug
Obkom—oblast Party committee
Oblast—administrative region; see "krai"
Oblispolkom—oblast executive committee; see "ispolkom"
Okrug—electoral district
PF—popular front
Raiispolkom—raion executive committee; see "ispolkom"
Raikom—raion Party committee
Raion—administrative district; subdivision of an oblast, krai, or city
RSFSR—Russian Soviet Federated Socialist Republic
Sajudis—Lithuanian Restructuring Movement
Sejm—Assembly of the Lithuanian Restructuring Movement

SSR—Soviet Socialist Republic
SupSov—Supreme Soviet
TO—territorial okrug
USSR—Union of Soviet Socialist Republics
VASKhNIL—V. I. Lenin All-Union Academy of Agricultural Sciences

Note on Transliteration and Spelling of Names

In order to simplify references and indexing, names have been transliterated directly from Russian. For ease in reading, name endings that are sometimes transliterated as "skii" or "ski" have been given here as "sky." The Russian characters "e" and "ё" have been transliterated as "e." Soft and hard signs have been omitted throughout.

Names of delegates from those areas of the European USSR that use Latin script, however—notably the Baltic states and, now, Moldavia— have been rendered in their original language with the transliterated Russian version added in parentheses. These names are indexed under both spellings.

Part I

THE USSR'S NEW LEGISLATIVE BODIES

1

"All Power to the Soviets"?

At the Nineteenth All-Union Communist Party Conference in June 1988, a resolution on political reform was adopted that called for the creation of a totally new state body—the USSR Congress of People's Deputies (CPD)—and the election of a revamped Supreme Soviet (SupSov).[1] Almost exactly one year later, the founding sessions of these new legislative bodies were held. The Soviet Union had taken an important step forward in the process of democratization.

The economist Leonid Abalkin described the work of the CPD as "simply fantastic—unthinkable not just five but even one year ago." The Congress, Abalkin went on, "revealed the whole spectrum of opinions . . . in the country; it was a mirror reflecting the real situation in our society. It laid bare the distribution of forces between renewal and stagnation, the national ferment, the unresolved ecological questions, the intolerable accumulation of social problems—including that of poverty on a mass scale."[2]

At the close of the Supreme Soviet's first convocation, newly elected chairman of the Supreme Soviet Mikhail Gorbachev warmly evaluated its work.[3] The new legislature, he said, had laid "a sound foundation" for the creation of "a socialist law-governed state," established "the political preconditions" necessary for combining socialism and democracy, and rendered *perestroika* irreversible. The Supreme Soviet, he asserted, had proved itself "an authoritative link in our self-renewing political system."

It is nevertheless still too early to know what precise impact the new legislative institutions will have on the Soviet political process. They had, at the time of writing, only just held their opening sessions. Relationships between the various branches of government—the CPD, the Supreme Soviet, and the commissions and committees attached to the Supreme Soviet's two chambers—were not at all clearly defined. These questions occupied a central position at the opening sessions of the Congress and Supreme Soviet. Although some progress was made in working them out, they had not been completely resolved at the time this book was in preparation. A figure graphically presenting the relationships among the CPD, the Supreme Soviet, and the government—insofar as they are known—can be found at the end of Part I, on pages 38 and 39.

Most important of all, relations between the legislative institutions and the Communist Party (CPSU) were murkily defined. Although certain duties, rights, and responsibilities were assigned to the legislature, the question of where ultimate power and authority lay was still undecided. Granted that changes had been made to the USSR Constitution and that more were promised for 1990, Article 6—which describes the CPSU as "the guiding and directing force in Soviet society, the nucleus of its political system and of all state and social organizations"—still remains in force, even though calls for its abolition have been heard.

On the most banal level, parliamentary procedures were inchoate or nonexistent. Soviet commentators criticized the fact that, in addressing the Congress, many deputies sought to harangue rather than to convince the audience. Speakers made interesting and even valuable proposals that were overlooked because there was no mechanism for putting suggestions to the vote. People's deputies in the USSR lacked many of the backup services upon which U.S. congressmen or British members of Parliament rely to accomplish their tasks. During the summer of 1989, however, steps were taken to provide Soviet parliamentarians with greater access to information sources.[4] Work was also under way to install an electronic voting system in the halls where the Supreme Soviet meets, the aim being to speed up the process of vote counting, to enable deputies to cast their votes out of the eagle-eye of their delegation leader, and to enable constituents to determine how their representatives voted on a given issue.[5]

It is fair to say that the Soviet leaders were no longer making any claim to having built a perfect democratic system. They said only that their political system is undergoing a process of "democratization" and they themselves are passing through "the school of democracy." Where these changes are leading is still unknown. The old rules that governed the Soviet political game are changing, but the contours of the new system and the rules by which the new game will be played are still unclear—and not just to outsiders.

Background

Mikhail Gorbachev began publicly mentioning the need for changes in the functions of the soviets (the organs of local government) at the Twenty-seventh Communist Party Congress in 1986. At that time he noted that proposals were being developed "to enhance the soviets' autonomy and activity." At that Congress, too, a new version of the Party

Rules was adopted in which an attempt was made to draw more clearly the lines separating the Party, the government, and the state.[6]

At a plenum of the CPSU Central Committee (CC) in January 1987, Gorbachev focused more specifically on the need for changes in political institutions. The causes of the Soviet economic crisis lay not only in subjective errors made under Leonid Brezhnev's leadership, he said, but also in "serious shortcomings in the performance of the institutions of Socialist democracy." Gorbachev proposed that Party secretaries, including first secretaries, should be elected in multicandidate, secret ballot elections and that more non-Party personnel should be in leading posts in the government and the economy. This was also the plenum at which Gorbachev first called for the convening of a CPSU conference.[7]

As the date of the Party conference approached, a number of proposals concerning reform of the Soviet political system were put forward.[8] There was widespread agreement on the need to extricate the Party from day-to-day involvement in economic affairs and, in connection with this, many proposals advocated granting greater authority to the soviets and to economic managers. The Central Committee Theses, a document issued in advance of the Party conference to show the direction in which the Party wanted the discussion to go, reflected these issues.[9]

The Theses acknowledged that the rights and powers of the soviets had been curtailed and their powers usurped by both Party committees and ministries. "All specific questions of state, economic, social, and cultural life" should, according to the Theses, be decided by the soviets. With respect to the Supreme Soviet, the Theses advised that its authority "grow radically." Various recommendations were put forward, including holding longer sessions, delimiting the specific powers of each of the Supreme Soviet's two chambers, electing deputies to represent public organizations, limiting deputies to two five-year terms, prohibiting anyone from belonging to more than two soviets simultaneously, and holding multicandidate, secret ballot elections.

In his opening speech to the delegates to the June 1988 Party conference, Gorbachev sketchily outlined possible changes in the structure and functions of the soviets of people's deputies at both the all-Union and local levels.[10] Many of the suggestions made by the general secretary were expected, having been foreshadowed in the Theses and in proposals aired in the Soviet media. His suggestion that a Congress of People's Deputies be created was, however, a complete surprise.

2

Structure of the USSR's New Legislative System

The Congress of People's Deputies

In accordance with the resolutions adopted at the Party conference, a number of constitutional amendments were adopted in December 1988, together with a law governing the election of deputies to the Congress of People's Deputies. These amendments state that the Congress is the "supreme organ of USSR state power" with the authority to examine and decide "any question within the jurisdiction of the USSR."[11] The law also assigns specific tasks to the Congress. These include

- adopting and amending the USSR Constitution;
- adopting decisions on questions of the national-state structure within the jurisdiction of the USSR;
- defining the USSR state border and ratifying border changes between Union republics;
- defining the basic guidelines of USSR foreign and domestic policy;
- ratifying long-range state plans and significant all-Union programs for the economic and social development of the USSR;
- electing the USSR Supreme Soviet, the chairman of the USSR Supreme Soviet, and the first deputy chairman of the USSR Supreme Soviet;
- confirming the chairman of the Council of Ministers, the chairman of the USSR People's Control Committee, the chairman of the USSR Supreme Soviet, the USSR prosecutor general, and the USSR chief state arbiter;
- electing the USSR Constitutional Oversight Committee;
- repealing acts adopted by the USSR Supreme Soviet;
- adopting decisions on holding nationwide referenda.

According to the amended Constitution, the Congress was to convene once a year. At its first convocation, however, the deputies voted to hold biannual sessions. The amendment further stipulates that laws and resolutions are adopted by a majority of votes of the total number of deputies.

The 2,250 members of the Congress are elected once every five years. There are some restrictions on who can be elected to the Congress (and, therefore, to the Supreme Soviet). With the exception of the chairman of the USSR Council of Ministers (who is the prime minister of the USSR), members of the USSR Council of Ministers, judges, and state arbiters at the all-Union level may not stand for election to the CPD. People who are mentally ill, those deemed incompetent by the court, those serving prison sentences, and anyone serving in a compulsory treatment center cannot serve as a Congress deputy. Otherwise, any citizen aged 21 or older may be elected as a USSR people's deputy, but no one may be a member of more than two soviets simultaneously.

All deputies are limited to two five-year terms. Deputies who "fail to justify the trust of voters" may be recalled at any time by a decision of the majority of the constituents in their okrug (electoral district) or in the organization that elected them.

Fifteen hundred members of the CPD are chosen according to territorial and national criteria; the other 750 represent Party, trade union, cooperative, youth, women's, veterans', scientific, and other organizations "established in accordance with the procedure laid down by law and having all-Union or republic organs." The latter requirement seems designed to prevent members of the USSR's more than 30,000 informal groups from advancing their own candidates to the Congress, though it does not prevent such people from seeking election as a representative of a territorial or national-territorial okrug.

The 1,500 territorial and national-territorial seats are distributed on the following basis: 750 seats are assigned to territorial okrugs with 257,300 voters each, while 750 seats are divided between Union republics (32 from each), autonomous republics (11 from each), autonomous oblasts (5 from each), and autonomous okrugs (1 from each).

The Supreme Soviet

According to the law amending the USSR Constitution, the Supreme Soviet is convened annually by its Presidium for two sessions—spring and fall—each lasting from three to four months. Supreme Soviet sessions take a variety of forms. Each chamber may sit separately or there may be joint sittings of both chambers—the Council of the Union and the Council of Nationalities. Sittings of the permanent commissions attached to each chamber as well as sittings of the committees attached to the Supreme Soviet are also considered conventions of the Supreme Soviet Sessions are opened and closed, however, by separate or joint sittings of both chambers.

As is the case with the Congress, certain responsibilities rest with the Supreme Soviet. These include

- scheduling elections of USSR people's deputies and ratifying the composition of the Central Electoral Commission;
- appointing the chairman of the USSR Council of Ministers, ratifying the composition of the USSR Council of Ministers as suggested by its chairman, and creating or abolishing USSR ministries and state committees;
- forming the USSR Defense Council and ratifying its composition and its appointments to the supreme command of the USSR Armed Forces;
- electing the USSR People's Control Committee and the USSR Supreme Court;
- appointing the USSR general prosecutor and the USSR chief state arbiter and ratifying the membership of the collegiums of the USSR Prosecutor's Office and the USSR State Board of Arbitration;
- holding regular hearings on the performance of those bodies and officials appointed or elected by the Supreme Soviet;
- implementing legislative regulations governing property relations, organization of the management of the national economy, social and cultural development, the budget and financial system, labor remuneration and price formation, taxation, environmental protection, and the utilization of natural resources;
- organizing the procedure for realization of the constitutional rights, freedoms, and duties of citizens;
- outlining general principles of the organization and activity of republic and local organs of state power and administration and determining the legal status of social organizations;
- interpreting USSR laws;
- submitting draft long-range plans and significant programs for economic and social development to the CPD for ratification, ratifying state plans and the state budget, monitoring progress in the implementation of the plans and budget, ratifying reports on their progress, introducing amendments to the plans and budget when necessary;
- ratifying and nullifying the USSR's international treaties;

- overseeing the granting of loans and other economic aid to foreign countries and concluding agreements on state loans and credits from foreign sources;
- determining basic measures in defense and state security, proclaiming full or partial mobilization, proclaiming a state of war in the event of an armed attack on the USSR or in the event of need to meet international treaty obligations, and taking decisions regarding the deployment of Soviet armed forces contingents in the event of the need to meet international treaty obligations;
- establishing USSR orders and medals and conferring honorary titles of the USSR;
- promulgating all-Union acts of amnesty;
- repealing resolutions and decrees of the USSR Supreme Soviet Presidium, orders of the chairman of the Supreme Soviet, and resolutions and orders of the USSR Council of Ministers;
- repealing resolutions and orders of republican councils of ministers if they are in violation of the USSR Constitution and laws;
- taking decisions on other issues, apart from those falling within the exclusive jurisdiction of the CPD.

The Supreme Soviet can adopt laws and resolutions; these must not run contrary to laws and other acts adopted by the Congress.

The Chairman

Extensive powers are vested in the chairman of the Supreme Soviet, "the highest official of the Soviet state." He signs all laws adopted by the Congress, the Supreme Soviet, and the Presidium of the Supreme Soviet and generally supervises the work of these bodies. The chairman nominates his first deputy chairman; the chairmen of the Council of Ministers, the People's Control Committee, and the Supreme Court; and the USSR general prosecutor and USSR chief state arbiter. He heads the Defense Council, conducts talks, signs international treaties of the USSR, and "issues orders." He reports to the Congress and the Supreme Soviet on the state of the Union and on other important questions of defense, foreign policy, and domestic affairs.

The chairman's powers are not without limits, however. He is subject to recall by the CPD at any time and certain of his actions are subject to approval by the Congress and the Supreme Soviet.

The Presidium

Eighteen Supreme Soviet officials are ex officio members of the Presidium. They include the chairman and first deputy chairman of the Supreme Soviet, the chairmen of both chambers and the People's Control Committee, and the chairmen of the standing commissions and committees of the Supreme Soviet.

The Presidium is charged with convening the Supreme Soviet, preparing for sittings of the Congress and the Supreme Soviet, coordinating the activities of the commissions and committees, assisting deputies with the exercise of their powers, and publishing—in the languages of the Union republics—all laws and other acts adopted by the Congress and the Supreme Soviet and its chambers, Presidium, and chairman. It is also responsible for ensuring that the constitutions and laws adopted by the republics comply with the Constitution of the USSR, for conferring the highest military titles and diplomatic ranks, for granting citizenship and resolving questions of the renunciation or deprivation of citizenship or asylum, for granting pardons, and for the appointment and recall of Soviet diplomatic representatives in foreign countries. The Presidium can declare a state of martial law or emergency in any region or nationwide and introduce special forms of administration.

The Presidium can also issue decrees and adopt resolutions. When the Supreme Soviet is not in session, the Presidium can declare a general or partial mobilization or a state of war.

The Council of the Union and the Council of Nationalities

The Supreme Soviet has two chambers. The first, the Council of the Union, focuses on questions of socioeconomic and state development of general importance for the entire Soviet Union and on questions of the rights, freedoms, and duties of Soviet citizens. It is concerned with Soviet foreign policy, defense, and state security.

The second, the Council of Nationalities, is charged with ensuring national equality and protecting the interests of nations, nationalities, and ethnic groups in accordance with the general interests of the Soviet Union. It also regulates interethnic relations.

The 271 members of the Council of the Union are elected by the CPD from among those of its members who represent territorial okrugs or public organizations. The amendment to the Constitution stipulates that the number of voters in the Union republics or regions should be taken into account when electing deputies to the Council of the Union.

The Council of Nationalities also contains 271 members, elected by the Congress from among those of its members who represent national-territorial okrugs or public organizations. Eleven deputies are elected from each Union republic, four from each autonomous republic, two from each autonomous oblast, and one from each autonomous okrug.

The Deputies

Any deputy may initiate legislation. At sittings of the Congress and Supreme Soviet a deputy has the right to put oral or written questions to the chairman of the Supreme Soviet, to any member of the USSR Council of Ministers, and to the heads of any organization elected or appointed by the Congress or the Supreme Soviet. The organ or official to whom the inquiry is put must respond before the Congress adjourns or at the given session of the Supreme Soviet within three days.

Deputies cannot be subjected to criminal proceedings, arrest, or the imposition of administrative penalties without the consent of the USSR Supreme Soviet. Deputies elected to the Supreme Soviet can be released from their other jobs for the duration of their membership. All deputies are released from the performance of their other functions while the Congress or the Supreme Soviet and its chambers, commissions, and committees are in session, and while working with constituents. "As a rule," deputies exercise their powers without permanently relinquishing their other official functions or employment.

Deputies are required to report to their constituents on their work and on the work of the Congress (and the Supreme Soviet or its committees and commissions if they are a member of them). Deputies who do not fulfill their constituents' mandates are subject to recall.

At the opening session of the Congress some debate concerned the possibility that deputies not elected to the Supreme Soviet might somehow be relegated to a lesser role. As a result of the debate, the Congress adopted a document outlining, in provisional form, the status of a people's deputy.[12] (A law on the status of people's deputies was scheduled for adoption in the fourth quarter of 1989, during the second session of the Congress.) The document reiterates some of the rights expounded in the constitutional amendment—for example, the right to inquiry and to introduce legislation—and clarifies others. Among the latter is the right of any deputy to attend any session of the Supreme Soviet, its chambers, commissions, and committees. Deputies who do not belong to the Supreme Soviet are entitled to a consultative vote at joint sessions, at sessions of either chamber, or at meetings of the comittees or commissions.

The document also states that membership in the Supreme Soviet is not a requirement for membership in the committees or commissions attached to the Supreme Soviet. Although the resolution does not explicitly say so, it was decided at the Congress that 50 percent of the members of each committee and commission should be Congress deputies who do not belong to the Supreme Soviet.

A number of practical steps connected with the establishment of a permanent deputy corps also had to be taken. With apartments in Moscow at a premium, one of the most important questions was, where would the deputies live? Such questions were not seriously addressed by the authorities before the Congress convened. Instead, the officials concerned repeatedly insisted that everything would be decided at the Congress' first session. The result of their decision was that, for the foreseeable future, Supreme Soviet deputies will be living in hotels.[13]

A deputy is entitled to a helper-secretary, who must be a staff member of a state enterprise or institution or work for a local ispolkom. The state will pay this expense (whether from central or local funds is not explained). Deputies have the right to library resources, the means of communication, and office space while participating in the work of the Congress and the Supreme Soviet and its committees and commissions. They also have the right to space for receiving constituents and fulfilling their duties at their place of residence.

It has been proposed that deputies be paid 200 rubles per month while the Congress sits. Deputies who relinquish other jobs while serving in the Supreme Soviet will receive 500 rubles per month and are guaranteed the right of return either to their old job or to another at a comparable salary level once their work in the Supreme Soviet is over.

In a one-sentence aside in his speech to the Party conference, Gorbachev remarked that a good deal of thought had been given to the question of a periodic renewal of part of the Supreme Soviet, but he did not make clear how this might be achieved. The law on amendments to the Constitution states that one-fifth of the membership of each of the chambers of the Supreme Soviet is renewed annually but it does not specify how this is to be done. The question was not debated at the Congress's first session, although several deputies did remark, in connection with the elections to the Supreme Soviet, that there would be rotation.

3

Elections to the Congress of People's Deputies

How democratic are the CPD and Supreme Soviet? How close do the USSR's new parliamentary bodies come to "representative democracy," that is, to a system of government under which citizens have the right to participate in political decision making, exercising this right not in person but through representatives chosen by and responsible to them? Under such a system, accountability is guaranteed through regular elections at which the population can vote the government out of office. To ensure that the electorate is presented with a real choice, representatives of at least two political parties stand for election.

Does the Congress of People's Deputies meet these criteria? Clearly it does not. Soviet democracy is still a long way away from Western concepts of democracy—even though the elections held in spring 1989 were the first nationwide multicandidate elections in the USSR since 1917 and, as observed by reformist magazine editor Vitalii Korotich, the new electoral system was a vast improvement on the old one. But consider the way in which the 2,250 members of the Congress of People's Deputies were elected. To start with, one-third of the deputies were not elected by the general public, but nominated by various establishment institutions, many of them dominated by the Communist Party. The fundamental Western principle of "one man, one vote" was not observed. Ordinary people had one vote, but members of the elite had two or three.

Candidates were screened by local electoral commissions before their names could appear on the ballot: in some cases, these commissions excluded candidates considered "undesirable" by local bigwigs. (For details, see the sections on the elections in Moscow and Voronezh.) In the Baltic states, however, electoral commissions did not preselect candidates but registered all comers; as a result, the elections in those areas seem to have come closer to the democratic ideal.

The electorate was also deprived of a real choice by the Soviet Union's lack of a multiparty system. To be sure, the elections were innovative in that candidates went to the electorate for the first time with their own programs. In the absence of competing parties, however, this innovation should not be overestimated. Voters were offered a selection of candidates, the vast majority of whom professed a single party line. Conventional wisdom puts it well: without a choice between parties, voters can select individuals, but not a government.

In a quarter (399) of the electoral okrugs, voters were presented with a single candidate running unopposed. There were more single-candidate races in Kazakhstan and Uzbekistan than in any other republic. Elections in Leningrad, the Soviet Union's second largest city, showed, however, that running a single candidate race can be a double-edged weapon in the hands of a sophisticated electorate. On March 26, in the first round of elections, voters there rejected Party boss Yurii Solovev—a candidate member of the Politburo—and five other top city leaders in a crushing defeat that reverberated throughout the Party organization. Just as in Poland earlier (although on a smaller scale), the determined use of negative voting in Leningrad, showed how an unfree election can be turned into one that is virtually free.

Again, the picture was different in the Baltic states. There the elections were not merely multicandidate but virtually multiparty. In Lithuania the republic's Popular Front (the Lithuanian Restructuring Movement, Sajudis) won an overwhelming victory. Sajudis ran candidates in almost all electoral wards and almost all its candidates won their races. Only where Sajudis withdrew its candidates did Lithuanian Communist Party leaders manage to win election, that is, their election was shown to be the movement's gift. In this way, Sajudis demonstrated that, only a year after its inception, it had become the main political force in the republic.

Finally, although few reports appeared in the official media, rumors of ballot rigging circulated, and numerous complaints of skulduggery were voiced prior to the elections. Sajudis complained, for example, that local officials had prevented it from printing its election posters and leaflets, while wide-scale electoral malpractice was alleged in Moldavia, where unofficial candidates were denied authorization for electoral meetings, voters were intimidated, and threats were made against campaign workers.[14] When the Congress met, the chairman of the Credentials Commission acknowledged that complaints had been lodged and said the Central Electoral Commission had received over 8,000 letters and about 1,000 visits from citizens. He did not specify how many of these were complaints. He affirmed, however, that members of the public had complained about the "unequal access to the mass media" given to various candidates, "attempts to put pressure on voters," and "unjustified refusal to register candidates."[15]

The Case of Moscow

The elections in Moscow's 27 okrugs were less democratic than those in the Baltic republics but were, in the end, more democratic than those in many other places. The problems that arose in Moscow during the course of the election campaign were representative of the problems experienced in many other regions. In fact, leaving aside the extremes of the Baltic and Central Asian republics, Moscow's experience was fairly typical. For that reason, it is discussed here in detail.

Nomination and Registration Meetings

Individuals could be nominated in a variety of ways: they could nominate themselves or they could be nominated by workers' collectives, a group of neighborhood residents, or a public or professional organization. They could be nominated for a territorial seat, a national-territorial seat, or one of the seats allocated to public and professional organizations. The number of nominations a candidate received was a fairly reliable guide to the popularity or power of a particular candidate. A number of reformist candidates were nominated repeatedly in Moscow; Boris Eltsin, for example, was nominated in eleven Moscow okrugs, Yurii Afanasev and Andrei Sakharov in four, and Roy Medvedev in two. But securing a nomination was not always an easy process, as Vitalii Korotich's experience illustrates.

Korotich, the editor of the controversial weekly *Ogonek*, had been nominated by five groups as of early January 1989: the worker's collective of the Sakhalin Geophysics Expedition; the Dubin Raion Party organization; the Institute of Slavic and Balkan Studies and the Institute of Philosophy, both of the USSR Academy of Sciences; and the Estonian Journalists' Union.

In early January a group of residents of the Dzerzhinsky and Sverdlovsk Okrugs in Moscow also tried to nominate Korotich but failed. Although the hall held 800 people (and was reportedly full more than 40 minutes before the meeting was supposed to start) only 373 registered voters from the Dzerzhinsky and Sverdlovsk Okrugs were present—considerably fewer than the required minimum of 500. The meeting was, in essence, over when from the balcony members of the extreme Russian nationalist group Pamyat (Memory) suddenly began shouting derogatory statements concerning Korotich. The meeting ended in scuffles.[16]

On January 24, the last day remaining for nominations, another meeting was held. With 995 registered voters of the Sverdlovsk Okrug present, there was no need to worry about meeting the minimum quota. Just one hour before the midnight deadline, 787 votes for Korotich were counted. (As it happened, Korotich was in the United States at the time.) Once again, members of Pamyat were in the hall; this time, when they raised their banners, they were booed.[17]

Having been nominated, the "candidate candidate deputies" then had to undergo a candidate registration meeting. These meetings were conducted by local electoral commissions whose primary aim in many instances seemed to be to reduce the number of contenders to a maximum of two. Twenty-two candidate registration meetings were held in the city of Moscow (as compared to two in the Belorussian SSR and none in Latvia and Estonia, where every name was put on the ballot). The voters in three Moscow okrugs—Gagarin (with twelve candidates), Voroshilov (six), and Tushino (five)—persuaded the electoral commissions to include on the March 26 ballot the names of everyone who had been nominated. Prior to these registration meetings there were over 200 nominees; after the meetings, 82 candidate deputies, divided among 27 okrugs, remained.[18]

Korotich was one of those who did not survive his registration meeting. The Sverdlovsk Okrug electoral commission called a registration meeting on February 21 that lasted ten hours. Korotich and another contender (there were seven all told) walked out of the meeting when the chairman refused to recognize a majority demand for all seven names to be entered on the ballot. Reportedly, dozens of demonstrators with placards calling for the registration of all the candidates were outside.[19] Korotich did eventually win election to the Congress of People's Deputies—but from an okrug in Ukraine, not Moscow.

Things did not go smoothly in Moscow's Lenin Okrug either. The registration meeting lasted over ten hours, with 622 registered voters present to decide the fate of 12 nominees (including Gavriil Popov, Aleksei Emelyanov, Valerii Savitsky, Evgenii Evtushenko, and Anatolii Kiselev). In the end, Savitsky, who is a jurist, and Emelyanov, a writer, emerged victorious. Kiselev, director of the Khrunichev Machine Tool Factory, whom Popov classified as a member of the "military-industrial complex," was obviously the local Party committee's favorite. He had managed to secure nominations at 18 plants (Kiselev was the chairman of the local council of factory directors and seemingly he was able to persuade his colleagues to exercise their influence over their employees), so he had the largest block of supporters—108—at the meeting. But he was defeated: only 292 people voted for him, while 309 votes were cast against his candidacy.[20]

The Course of the Campaign

The media played a major role in the elections, stimulating popular interest and alerting members of the public to the issues at stake. A local Moscow TV show "Good Evening, Moscow!" invited every candidate to make an appearance during the weeks before the election. Not all of the candidates accepted this offer, which may have been a mistake on their part: one survey indicated that 70 percent of the voters polled relied on the show as their primary source of information about the elections.[21]

Although the election law set out rather specific rules concerning the conduct of campaigns, almost from the very beginning complaints were being heard.[22] Some candidates, by virtue of their positions, had greater access to resources. For example, Petr Surov, the chief of the Moscow City Construction Committee, had full-color leaflets and posters printed up and his supporters recommended that he repair potholes and fix street lamps in his okrug "so as to endear himself to his constituents."[23] Evgenii Brakov, the director of the ZIL Automobile Factory, was reportedly ferrying supporters to and from meetings in a fleet of ZIL autos, and so on.

Winners and Losers

There were no unopposed candidates in Moscow. In 15 okrugs there were only two contenders vying for a seat, but in the Gagarin Okrug 12 nominees battled for one seat, while in the 11 remaining okrugs anywhere from three to six people were registered to run.[24]

Surprisingly, only four Party and government officials managed to secure a place for themselves on a Moscow ballot—the second secretary of the Moscow city Party committee, Yurii Prokofev; two first secretaries of raion Party committees; and the chairman of the Moscow city ispolkom, Valerii Saikin. Nine of the candidate deputies were workers, which was fewer than in past elections, but the number of managers rose considerably in comparison with past elections. Only five women were nominated. The candidates ranged in age from 29 to 68. A number of intellectuals, for example, Roy Medvedev, the author of several important historical works, and Yurii Chernichenko, known for his frank and sharp analysis of agricultural problems, were nominated, as was senior investigator Telman Gdlyan, who had become a popular hero as a result of his investigation into corruption in Uzbekistan and his allegation that Egor Ligachev and other Politburo members were implicated in corruption scandals. (Ligachev indignantly denied the charge.)

The first round of elections was held on March 26. In Moscow, 16 contenders won the first time around, including Boris Eltsin, who garnered 89 percent of the vote (with 84 percent of those eligible voting) and Telman Gdlyan, who easily defeated four other contestants by winning 86.8 percent of the vote in his okrug. Runoff elections were held in eight okrugs on April 9. New elections were held in three additional okrugs in which none of the candidates received the necessary 50 percent minimum of votes cast. Following a first round of elections, all three of these okrugs had to hold runoff elections, so that the "election marathon," which began in March, did not finally end in Moscow until May 19. The three okrugs that held new elections had originally registered just two candidates for each seat; in the new elections, they registered seven, nine, and ten contenders respectively. This was a common pattern throughout the Soviet Union in the case of new elections—rather than limit the number, essentially everyone was registered. In turn, this practice led to the need for yet another round of runoff elections. (The rules were also slightly different for runoff elections; the candidate merely had to defeat his or her opponent, rather than garner at least 50 percent of the votes cast.)

Voter turnout in the Moscow elections held on March 26 was good, with all okrugs reporting between 78 and 86 percent turnout. In the runoff elections held on April 9, voter turnout was lower, but still respectable, averaging about 67 percent. It is almost impossible to determine who stayed away from the elections, although a survey of young adults (age 18-30) provides a small clue. Thirty-one percent of those asked said that they could see no difference between the new system of elections and the old; 16 percent said they simply were not interested in elections at all. Sixty-two percent said they were planning to vote on March 26; 15 percent said they were not.[25] Another survey, conducted on March 25—a day before the elections—found that 28 percent of those polled could not name even one of the candidates running in their okrug, 40 percent could name one, and 32 percent could name them all. These percentages look good when compared with the fact that 97 percent of those polled could not remember the name of their current representative in the Supreme Soviet![26]

Among the more famous winners in Moscow, in addition to those already mentioned, were Ilya Zaslavsky, a disabled young man whose platform included increased benefits for the handicapped; economist Oleg Bogomolov; historian Sergei Stankevich; and former Olympic weightlifting champion Yurii Vlasov. Well-known candidates who lost include legal expert Valerii Savitsky; Colonel General Dmitrii Volkogonov, author of a biography of Stalin; and playwright Mikhail Shatrov. The commander of the Moscow antiaircraft defenses, Vladimir Tsarkov, also lost.

Most striking, however, was the beating taken by the local establishment. Although the majority of Moscow's deputies turned out to be Party members (18, plus one candidate member), the four Party and government officials—Prokofev, Saikin, and two raion secretaries—were defeated. (The highest ranking Party official in Moscow, Moscow city Party Committee first secretary Lev Zaikov, was elected as part of the CPSU slate of candidates.) Nor did the representatives of Party committees in factories, schools, or other organizations succeed in winning.

Saikin's defeat was attributed by Soviet sources to widespread dissatisfaction among Muscovites with living conditions in Moscow, especially with regard to transportation and environmental pollution. Yurii Prokofev, the second secretary of the city Party committee, gave an interview to *Moscow News* in which he said that he realized almost from the start that he "had no chance of winning."[27] The reasons he gave included voters' dissatisfaction with the economy and "the low level of political culture," by which Prokofev seemed to mean the tendency of the voters to heap blame and criticism on local Party officials while turning a deaf ear to any explanation the officials had to offer.

Boris Eltsin v. Evgenii Brakov

The most widely publicized campaign in the Soviet Union and abroad was that of Boris Eltsin, the former Moscow Party boss whose outspoken call for speeding up the reforms led to his ouster from his post and from the Politburo in 1987. His victimization by the Party hierarchy made him wildly popular with the general public.

At the January 1989 Central Committee plenum, Eltsin's name was scratched from the Party's list of candidates, at which point people throughout the Soviet Union began to nominate him.[28] He was nominated in at least 50 okrugs, including Ligachev's home base of Tomsk, but chose to run for Moscow's national-territorial seat, which represents over five million voters.[29]

Eltsin used the rights available to him as a candidate to spread his message: he appeared on Moscow television, he hired halls, his platform was reprinted in newspapers throughout the Soviet Union, and he was lionized by the foreign press. At the Central Committee plenum in March 1989 he was charged with having deviated from the Party line in the course of his campaign speeches, and a special commission was set up to investigate the matter—which seemed only to increase Eltsin's popularity with the voters.[30]

The registration meeting for Moscow's national-territorial seat lasted 13 hours. A total of 15 people were nominated; when it was over, only Eltsin and ZIL factory director Evgenii Brakov remained. Before the meeting, two people, one of whom was Politburo member Vitalii Vorotnikov, withdrew in order to run in other okrugs and three—including Andrei Sakharov—withdrew altogether (although Sakharov later was elected as a representative of the USSR Academy of Sciences). Brakov received 577 of the 875 votes cast at the meeting; Eltsin got 532.[31]

The campaign battle between Eltsin and Brakov was dramatic. Eltsin alleged that Brakov's supporters had tried to intimidate him with threatening telephone calls and attacks on his car.[32] On national television, one of Eltsin's supporters, the journalist Mikhail Poltoranin (who was himself elected a deputy), accused the Moscow Party apparatus of trying to manipulate the local media to swing the election against Eltsin.[33] One attempt to quiet Eltsin backfired: Moscow city government officials, without notifying anyone, reversed an earlier decision to permit a rally of Eltsin supporters—which led to a spontaneous rally of between 7,000 and 10,000 Muscovites in front of the city's Executive Committee headquarters.[34]

As election day approached, Moscow residents took to the streets, holding rallies in support of Eltsin. On March 18, eight days before the election, about 7,000 people turned out for a campaign meeting in a Moscow suburb to hear Eltsin speak.[35] The next day, roughly 3,000 Eltsin supporters, who were by this time afraid that the election returns might be manipulated, declared their intention to call a one-day strike if Eltsin did not win the election.[36]

Eltsin won a landslide victory, garnering just under 90 percent of the votes cast, which gave him something no other Soviet politician has ever been able to claim: a popular mandate gained in (what was almost) a democratic election. Vitalii Tretyakov, a political analyst with *Moscow News*, attempted an analysis of "the Eltsin phenomenon." He offered his answer to a question that had been posed by *Pravda* in an editorial on the election results: "Why does a Party committee's dislike of a deputy with whom the apparatus doesn't sympathize suddenly give rise to powerful support from the people?" The reason, Tretyakov wrote, was that people identified with Eltsin:

> He is a victim of dislike on the part of the higher-ups—who of us hasn't been in the same position? And he is being slighted for refusing to look for their approval—who hasn't dreamed of doing this?[37]

The Case of Voronezh Oblast

The ease with which the electoral regulations could be used by unscrupulous officials to flout the popular will was highlighted by Soviet television in a detailed report from the Rossosh Okrug of Central Russia's Voronezh Oblast. There, after local Party officials failed to win election to the CPD in the first round of elections on March 26, the well-known television journalist Aleksandr Tikhomirov was nominated by workers at 92 local work collectives to run as a candidate in fresh elections to be held in May. Tikhomirov recorded his electoral campaign on film; after local officials managed to get his name excluded from the ballot, he screened his report on prime-time Soviet television.[38]

As a charismatic outsider, supported by local people because they thought he could represent their point of view in the corridors of power and because he had no association with the bosses they had refused to elect in the first round, Tikhomirov was fiercely resented by the Rossosh Party officials. His campaign soon developed into a vendetta between himself and the Rossosh Party boss, Ivan Timofeevich Kokotkin. Tikhomirov informed a public meeting that, "one hour after my arrival, Ivan Timofeevich summoned the Party *aktiv* and told them to tear up my leaflets and to hound the initiative groups [that had proposed my candidacy]."

The hostile reaction of the authorities only increased Tikhomirov's popularity with the local inhabitants, who turned out for his meetings in force. Refused permission to meet in public halls, they held election rallies in the open air. "Why are they turning me into the Rossosh

Eltsin?" Tikhomirov demanded at one public meeting; "Likened himself to Eltsin," a Party activist in the audience was seen to write in his notebook.

In the end, to put a stop to Tikhomirov's campaign the local officials had only to apply the letter, if not the spirit, of the electoral regulations. A meeting was held on April 15 to choose whose names should appear on the ballot. The meeting was attended not by the electorate but their "representatives," that is, local worthies—nominated to the electoral commission by Party functionaries—who voted not as the workers wanted but as the Party leaders told them. Members of the public stood outside with banners calling on the electoral commission to include on the ballot the names of all 12 candidates nominated by the local work collectives. That way, the electorate would have had a real choice on polling day. Instead, the electoral commission voted to include only four names. Needless to say, Tikhomirov's was not among them, and he was thereby deprived of the possibility to stand as a candidate. The final shot of Tikhomirov's film showed him promising his supporters that he would return to Moscow and fight for a reform of the electoral law.

4

Remaking the Supreme Soviet

Elections to the Council of the Union and the Council of Nationalities

One of the first tasks given to the Congress was the election of the two councils of the new Supreme Soviet. Even before the Congress convened, battles were being waged over the formation of the Supreme Soviet. A number of changes to the USSR Constitution were required and were hotly debated during the period following the 1988 Party conference.

The debates began in earnest on October 22, 1988, with the publication of the draft of proposed changes to the Constitution. The crux of the debate was nationality representation in the new legislative bodies and the possible restriction of the rights of the republics vis-à-vis those of Moscow. In the nationwide debate that followed the publication and at a session of the USSR Supreme Soviet held on October 28, 1988, a number of changes to the draft were proposed, many of which were incorporated into the final law adopted at a session of the USSR Supreme Soviet on November 29.[39]

Following the elections of the deputies to the Congress but before the opening of the Congress, regional conferences of deputies were held across the Soviet Union. At the time, very little information was released concerning these meetings, but their importance was evident from the participation of high-ranking Party officials in many of them.[40] Shortly before the Congress convened, it was learned that the purpose of the meetings was to determine who among the deputies would stand for election to the Supreme Soviet. At the Congress itself, however, many deputies complained either that they were not included in the meetings or that, in any case, it was the Party apparatus that decided whom to nominate.[41]

At one such meeting on May 22, chairman of the Presidium of the RSFSR Supreme Soviet Vitalii Vorotnikov presented a group of deputies from the RSFSR with a list of 147 Party-approved names for election to the Supreme Soviet.[42] The CPSU Central Committee had apparently ratified this list and presumably others like it at its closed-door meeting on May 21. At the urging of the Moscow deputies, the RSFSR deputies refused to approve the list, which included the names of several radical deputies but also those of many bureaucrats. What most annoyed the deputies, however, was the way these lists had been compiled. According to Sergei Stankevich, a member of the Moscow group, "many deputies never even knew they were selected. They were just appointed."[43]

Moscow News reported on May 18 that 450 deputies would be meeting in Moscow before the Congress to conduct a preliminary discussion of the agenda. The members of this group, known as the "Assembly of Representatives," were elected at the regional conferences of deputies mentioned above.[44] Their names were not made public, although a few deputies revealed in their speeches to the Congress that they participated in the Assembly meeting.[45] The Assembly, with 446 deputies present, met for nine hours on the day before the Congress opened to discuss a number of questions, including the agenda, the rules, and the lists of candidates nominated to serve in the Mandate Commission, the Supreme Soviet, and the Presidium of the CPD.[46]

At the Congress itself, much of the early debate concerned the lists of candidates to the Supreme Soviet, the procedure for voting on them, and the status of Supreme Soviet deputies. Interestingly enough, the deputies did not question the need for lists. They did argue heatedly about the need for equal representation of all nationality groups in the Council of the Union (whose membership is based on population), the way the lists of candidates had been drawn up, the merits of voting by republic, and the desirability of requiring Supreme Soviet deputies to resign from their other jobs.

Typical of the stories told at the Congress was that related by V. V. Gulii, a newspaper reporter from Sakhalin. Two deputies from Sakhalin were put on the list of candidates for the RSFSR, but some of the Sakhalin deputies—including one who had been nominated—knew nothing about the list until they heard it read it out at a meeting on May 22. "How did it come about that such a decision was taken?" Gulii asked. "Who dared to assume this responsibility? I think you have guessed—our boldest people—the apparatus workers."[47]

The organization of the deputies by region was the chief source of many of the complaints at the Congress. Throughout the election campaign, the Central Electoral Commission made it clear that it was categorizing the deputies according to territorial divisions (whose lines were generally drawn so as to coincide with nationality). The deputies were seated at the Congress in accordance with this principle, even if they had been elected as representatives of the journalists' union or the CPSU and regardless of their actual nationality. The deputies from Moscow were seated near the front of the hall; those from the Baltic, near the rear. The figures cited in the Mandate Commission's report to the Congress revealed how large each republic's contingent of deputies was; these figures are given below.[48] A deputy from Latvia later cited

RSFSR	1,099
Ukraine	262
Uzbekistan	108
Kazakhstan	99
Belorussia	94
Georgia	91
Azerbaijan	72
Lithuania	58
Tajikistan	57
Moldavia	55
Armenia	53
Kirgizia	53
Latvia	52
Estonia	48
Turkmenistan	48

the numerical superiority enjoyed by the RSFSR as a further reason for each republic to vote only for its own deputies to the Supreme Soviet.

Regional Representation in the Council of the Union

Some deputies argued against making regional affiliation an issue when deputies were chosen for the Council of the Union. S. N. Fedorov, chairman of the Soviet Charity Fund, told the deputies that they should not elect "defenders of some single region, some locality. The Council of Nationalities exists for that."[49] Another deputy sent a note to the Presidium asking: "What are we talking about? If the procedure for elections [to the Council of the Union] is the same as that for election to the Council of Nationalities, how will the former differ from the latter?"[50] But the problem, as Fedor Burlatsky pointed out, was that for many years the republics had been "under pressure from Moscow, from the center, and now, of course, they want to defend their interests."[51] The

Council of the Union will decide questions of all-Union importance; the potential obviously exists for those questions to be decided in a way that members of different nationality groups might consider harmful.

Many deputies, especially those from the RSFSR, were unhappy about the way the territorial lines determining representation in the Council of the Union were drawn. Grigorii Posibeev, Party first secretary in the Mari ASSR, told the Congress: "The fact that four autonomous republics do not have a single representative in the Council of the Union is clearly the result of a flaw in the system of elections to [the Council] from regions of the country and from national groupings." V. N. Zubkov, one of the deputies from Rostov region, asked how it was possible that Rostov-na-Donu, a city of more than one million inhabitants, had no candidate for the Supreme Soviet; "we need someone to protect the interests of the city," he said.[52]

Multiple Candidacies

The Moscow deputies were in favor of multiple candidacies, and they ultimately paid a high political price for standing by this principle. They nominated 55 candidates for 29 seats, and the result was that some of the best-known reformers were not elected to the Supreme Soviet. Other deputies were opposed to multiple candidacies precisely because the specter of defeat loomed before them. As one deputy explained:

> Take the RSFSR. Good lads. They put forward four extra people and displayed the principle of having alterna- tives. . . . But look at what happened in the voting . . . three oblast secretaries did not go through. That is why we have so insistently and stubbornly departed from the principle of having alternatives—because the situation in the country is now such that people connect every . . . shortcoming with the work of the leading bodies, which, I can assure you, are not always [to blame].[53]

The Baltic deputies chose not to nominate alternative candidates because they, too, feared defeat. In their case, however, they were con- cerned about the defeat not of Party leaders but of reformers. They therefore nominated only one deputy for each seat, so as to make it more difficult for conservative deputies to reject their candidates. (The Baltic deputies also benefited from the lack of *glasnost* in the USSR concerning events in the Baltic; many of the deputies were unfamiliar with the names of the most radical Baltic deputies.) They also argued for voting by republic, because they were afraid of their defeat in a vote of the entire Congress.

Full-Time Parliamentarians

Debate on who should be a Supreme Soviet deputy began well before the Congress convened. Many argued for professional politicians, but in the same breath said that such individuals were in short supply (it went without saying that professional Party *apparatchiki* were not the sort of individuals these people had in mind).[54]

There was a heated debate over the desirability of having Supreme Soviet deputies resign from their other positions so as to serve as full-time parliamentarians. Gorbachev ruled that deputies in the Supreme Soviet would not be required to give up their jobs, because such a restriction would limit participation in the Supreme Soviet. But many speakers disagreed and argued that it would be foolish to ask someone like an oblast Party committee first secretary to combine two jobs.

Vladimir P. Zolotukhin, a reporter for the military newspaper *Frunzevets* in Uzbekistan, said that among the deputies nominated to the Supreme Soviet from Uzbekistan were many of the republic's top officials, including the republican first secretary, the chairman of the Council of Ministers, the chairman of the republican planning committee, the chairman of the presidium of the republican Supreme Soviet, and three oblast Party committee first secretaries. "I am very worried," he said, "about how these comrades will combine their jobs."[55]

The Moscow group had asked its nominees to the Supreme Soviet to declare their willingness to resign from their current positions, but it was the only delegation known to have done so. Vladimir Kudryavtsev, director of the USSR Academy of Sciences Institute of State and Law, said many scientists had declined to run for the Supreme Soviet because they could not take that much time away from their work.[56] If the Congress had decided against allowing deputies to combine two jobs, this would, of course, have meant that Gorbachev would have had to choose between the presidency and the post of general secretary.

Birth of an Official Opposition

At the end of July, radical deputies met to form the Interregional Group of Deputies (MDG)—the first official opposition group formed in the Soviet Union since the 1920s. They claimed to have the support of some 400 duputies to the CPD and 90 members of the Supreme Soviet. Gavriil Popov, who with Boris Eltsin, Andrei Sakharov, and Yurii Afanasev was among the leaders of the new group, said its purpose was not to counterpose itself to the Supreme Soviet but to insist that the Supreme Soviet meet the demands of the electorate. Interviewed on Soviet television on July 29, historian Sergei Stankevich, another founding member, said the formation of different opinion groups was essential for the successful functioning of any parliament. He predicted the emergence of as many as five or six of these groups (he was careful not to use the word "parties") within the CPD and argued that the existence of such groupings would aid the elaboration of rational policies and reasonable compromises—such as had been lacking in Soviet policy formation to date. Asked by his interviewer why he and his colleagues do not prefer to work through the committees and commissions of the Congress and the Supreme Soviet, Stankevich said that these bodies have a vital role but that their deliberations tend to take place behind closed doors and therefore the ideas they generate remain within a narrow circle. The aim of the MDG, on the other hand, is to bring to the attention of Soviet parliamentarians and the public the widest possible range of policy options, thereby ensuring that the broadest, most informed debate will take place before important decisions are adopted.

5

The Social and Political Composition of the Congress of People's Deputies and the Supreme Soviet

How representative are the new parliamentary bodies? In the past, Supreme Soviet deputies were nominated from above in accordance with strict quotas. The replacement of this system by multicandidate elections resulted in a sharp drop in the proportion of workers, peasants, and women in the new Congress and in the Supreme Soviet which it elected.

The Congress of People's Deputies

In 1984, the last time the Supreme Soviet was elected by the old method, 32.5 percent of the deputies were workers (although, according to official figures published in 1987, workers in industry and on state farms form 61.8 percent of the overall population). Workers made up only 18.6 percent of those elected to the CPD in the elections of March 26, 1989 (having made up 23.7 percent of those who stood as candidates).[57]

In 1984, 16.1 percent of the deputies were kolkhoz members (as opposed to 12 percent of the population overall). On March 26, 1989, kolkhoz members made up 11.2 percent of those elected (having formed 9 percent of those standing as candidates). White-collar workers, therefore, far outnumbered blue-collar workers and peasants in the new CPD.

Similarly, women—who made up 53 percent of the overall population in 1987—formed 32.8 percent of the deputies elected in 1984. On March 26, 1989, 17.1 percent of those elected were female, although women made up only 15.8 percent of the candidates overall.

Communist Party members, on the other hand, fared much better on March 26, 1989, when 87.6 percent of those elected belonged to the Party, than they did in 1984, when 71.5 percent of the deputies were Party members. Those elected in 1989, however, included more low-ranking Party members and no fewer high Party officials than in the past.

The drop in worker representation was keenly debated at a plenum of the CPSU Central Committee on April 25, 1989. The Party leader of Azerbaijan complained about what he called the "inadmissibly small" numbers of worker and peasant deputies and suggested that in future they should be guaranteed a certain number of seats in the Congress—along the lines of the seats reserved for the CPSU and Komsomol.[58]

When the CPD first assembled, there was general agreement that its overall composition was conservative. On the basis of the votes taken in the first days of the Congress, historian Yurii Afanasev denounced what he called its "aggressively obedient majority."[59] Baltic deputies described themselves as part of a "democratic minority," and Tatyana Zaslavskaya said that, when the Congress opened, she calculated that its "radical-democratic wing" numbered no more than 200-300 of the 2,250 deputies.[60] The extremely hostile reception that Andrei Sakharov received when he tried to explain his stance on Afghanistan seemed to bear out these assumptions. Some observers noted, however, that there were a fair number of "blank checks" among the deputies, that is, people whose minds were open to being changed by argument. And, as the Congress progressed, the radical wing demonstrated that, while always a minority, on certain issues it could muster as much as 20 percent of the votes. Moreover, the "progressives" counted among their ranks a number of highly articulate and principled people. By the close, Zaslavskaya was saying she thought the radicals numbered "considerably more" than the 10 percent she had earlier supposed.[61]

The Supreme Soviet

Again, the initial consensus was that the composition of the new Supreme Soviet was at worst conservative and at best centrist or conformist. Yurii Afanasev denounced it as "Stalinist-Brezhnevite" as soon as it was elected. But, like the CPD, the Supreme Soviet showed that it was not, as progressives had feared, stacked with "idle functionaries," but was prepared to begin flexing its muscles. While it is true that the majority of deputies proved "moderate" or even "cautious" in their approach, a small nucleus of more radical deputies emerged who assumed a leading role in the deliberations of the new body.

A schematic breakdown of the professional and social composition of the Congress of People's Deputies and the Supreme Soviet is contained in tables 1 and 2.

Table 1   Professional Composition of the USSR Supreme Soviet, 1984 and 1989, and the Congress of People's Deputies (CPD), 1989, in percentages

	Supreme Soviet 1984	CPD 1989	Supreme Soviet 1989
Top political leadership	1.5%	0.7%	0.2%
Top and middle-level managerial personnel	40.0	39.8	32.8
Lower-level managerial personnel	6.6	25.3	35.3
Workers, collective farmers, and nonprofessional office employees	45.9	22.1	18.3
Intelligentsia	6.0	10.2	12.5
Military	3.7	4.0	1.8
KGB	1.1	0.4	0.2
Pensioners	n.a.	1.6	0.9
Priests	0.0	0.3	0.0

Source: Moscow News, No. 24, 1989; authors' files.

Note: Percentages for the military and KGB were calculated by the authors and added to official Soviet data; for this reason the columns do not total 100%. The figure for pensioners in 1984 was not given in the source although there certainly were pensioners in the Supreme Soviet at that time.

At its first session, which ended on August 5, the Supreme Soviet proved far more self-assertive than observers had predicted and appeared to be on the way to establishing itself as the country's chief policy-debating body. It grilled Prime Minister Ryzhkov's new cabinet (which included the first non-Party member ever to fill a ministerial post in the USSR, Nikolai Vorontsov, as chairman of the State Committee for Environmental Protection); it approved early demobilization from the

Table 2   Social and Professional Composition of the Congress of People's Deputies and the Supreme Soviet

Members of the CPSU

in the CPD	87.6 %
in the Council of the Union	88.5
in the Council of Nationalities	87.4

Deputies elected by the CPSU Central Committee

in the CPD	4.4 %
in the Council of the Union	4.4
in the Council of Nationalities	5.1

Deputies elected from territorial or national-territorial okrugs (i.e., not elected by public or professional organizations)

in the CPD	66.6 %
in the Council of the Union	65.6
in the Council of Nationalities	81.1

Women

in the CPD	17.0 %
in the Council of the Union	16.2
in the Council of Nationalities	20.2

army for 176,000 students; it conferred its blessing on the economic independence of Lithuania and Estonia; gave the Soviet Union's very first law on strikes its first reading; modified the law on state crimes; and promised to raise pensions. In July, at the height of a massive coal miners' strike and amid renewed ethnic violence in the Caucasus, the Supreme Soviet issued a national appeal, declaring that it was assuming full responsibility for the situation in the country and would monitor the work of government and state bodies.

Further examination reveals striking similarities between the composition of the CPD and the two chambers of the Supreme Soviet. Almost two-thirds of the members of the Council of the Union won their seats in national elections, whereas just over one-third were elected by a public, professional, or political organization such as the

CPSU, Komsomol, or trade unions. The fact that this and other proportions cited in the table correspond almost exactly to the proportions in the Congress of People's Deputies suggests that preselection of candidates was conducted with the conscious aim of achieving such a balance.

In the Council of Nationalities, however, the balance was not maintained, and barely 20 percent of its seats went to those elected to seats in the CPD by public or political organizations. The fact that a larger percentage of deputies in the Council of Nationalities had to win their seats in contested local elections suggests that this chamber may turn out to be slightly more radical than the Council of the Union, whose members seem to have been selected with the intention of replicating the social composition of the CPD. The Council of Nationalities does indeed appear to include a larger number of "radical" deputies than the Council of the Union. (This seems to be true, for example, of the Estonian and Moldavian deputies.) Nonetheless, "radicals" remain a minority in both chambers of the Supreme Soviet as they do in the CPD.

6

Conclusion

Each of Gorbachev's political reforms, viewed in isolation, fails to live up to Western notions of democracy—still the sum of the changes seems to be greater than the parts. A fragile system of checks and balances, a separation of powers between the Communist Party and the new Soviet parliament, is beginning to emerge. The new institutions seem eager to establish themselves as legitimate bodies, but they will first have to prove to the people that they are able to contribute to the peaceful resolution of the problems and conflicts troubling Soviet society.

Live media coverage of the activities of the Congress of People's Deputies and the Supreme Soviet had an enormous impact on the Soviet population. Even if the debate was often unfocused, the deputies still spoke their minds without fear, and no subject was off limits. The Soviet population saw its elected deputies—albeit imperfectly elected—assert their right to challenge the nation's rulers. A precedent was established; a dialogue was instituted; a bridge—no matter how flimsy—began to form between state and society, between the leaders and the led. When the coal miners of the Kuzbass went on strike in July, they said they had been emboldened by the debates they saw on television at the Congress and the Supreme Soviet: "Now it's our turn," they declared.

Notes

1. *Pravda*, July 5, 1988.
2. *Ekonomicheskaya gazeta*, No. 27, July 1989, p. 1.
3. Central Television, August 4, 1989.
4. "Informatsionnyi tsentr dlya parlamenta," *Izvestia*, August 29, 1989.
5. "Elektronika k uslugam parlamentariev," *Izvestia*, August 18, 1989.
6. TASS, February 25, 1986.
7. *Pravda*, January 28, 1987.
8. That which corresponded most closely to the system that eventually emerged was by Fedor Burlatsky; see his "O sovetskom parlamentarizme," *Literaturnaya gazeta*, June 15, 1988, p. 2.
9. TASS, May 26, 1988.
10. Central Television, June 28, 1988.
11. The full text was published in *Pravda*, December 3, 1988. The passages cited here were taken almost verbatim.
12. The draft was adopted on June 9 and released to the press on June 15, TASS, June 15, 1989 and Radio Moscow, June 15, 1989.
13. See, for example, *Komsomolskaya pravda*, February 28, 1989; *New Times*, May 1989, pp. 23-24; *Izvestia*, July 18, 1989.
14. Vladimir Socor, "Unofficial Groups Score Unexpected Gains in Elections in Moldavia," *Report on the USSR*, No. 19, 1989, pp. 17-20.
15. *Pravda*, May 26, 1989.
16. *Ogonek*, No. 3, January 14, 1989, p. 31; *Izvestia*, January 18, 1989.
17. AP, January 24, 1989; *Baltimore Sun*, January 25, 1989.
18. *Moscow News*, No. 6, 1989. For an account of the registration meeting in Tushino, see *Sotsialisticheskaya industriya*, February 16, 1989. For Western accounts of the hurly-burly of some Moscow nomination and registration meetings, see Knight-Ridder Newspapers, January 23, 1989; *Los Angeles Times*, March 16, 1989; *Guardian*, March 16, 1989; *Chicago Tribune*, February 26, 1989; Jonathan Coopersmith, "The March 26, 1989 Soviet Elections for the Congress of People's Deputies, Report of the Observers from the Center for Democracy" (unpublished), p. 6; *New York Times*, February 27, 1989; see also *Moscow News*, No. 6, 1989.
19. Reuters, February 22, 1989.
20. *New York Times*, February 12, 1989; see also *Moskovskie*

novosti, No. 8, 1989, p. 8.

    21. *Izvestia,* May 12, 1989.

    22. For a review of the rules governing election campaigns, see Dawn Mann, "Campaigning for Office in the Soviet Union," *Report on the USSR,* No. 10, 1989, pp. 5-7.

    23. *Moskovskie novosti,* No. 15, 1989, p. 9.

    24. TASS, February 28, 1989.

    25. *Moskovskie novosti,* No. 17, 1989, p. 8.

    26. *Moskovskie novosti,* No. 20, 1989, p. 9.

    27. *Moskovskie novosti,* No. 15, 1989, p. 9.

    28. *Guardian,* January 13, 1989.

    29. *Time,* March 23, 1989.

    30. Radio Moscow, March 16, 1989. The commission was quietly allowed to die without announcing any findings.

    31. AFP, February 10, 1989; *Sovetskaya Rossiya,* February 23, 1989; *Izvestia,* February 22, 1989.

    32. Reuters, March 12 and 20, 1989.

    33. "Vzglyad," Central Television, March 17, 1989. See also the devastating attack by Vladimir Tikhomirov (the Central Committee member who, at the Central Committee plenum in March, raised the question of Eltsin's deviation from the Party line) in *Moskovskaya pravda,* March 19, 1989.

    34. AP, March 19, 1989; *Izvestia,* March 20, 1989.

    35. Reuters, March 19, 1989.

    36. AP, March 19, 1989.

    37. *Moscow News,* No. 16, 1989, p. 10; *Pravda,* April 1, 1989.

    38. "Prozhektor perestroiki," Central Television, May 10, 1989.

    39. Ann Sheehy, "Upping Russian Representation in the Soviet Parliament," *RL Weekly Research Bulletin,* RL 474/88, October 31, 1988; Ann Sheehy, "Changes in Draft Law to Meet Baltic Objections?", *RL Weekly Research Bulletin,* RL 508/88, November 21, 1988; Ann Sheehy, "The Final Text of the Law on Amendments to the Constitution: Republican Rights," *RL Weekly Research Bulletin,* RL 553/88, December 12, 1988.

    40. On May 3, between 70 and 80 deputies in the Moscow area met with Gorbachev and recommended that he be nominated for the post of president (AP, May 3, 1989). Similar meetings were held in Ukraine, where Ukrainian Communist Party First Secretary Vladimir Shcherbitsky conducted the proceedings (Radio Moscow, May 11, 1989), and in Leningrad, where Vitalii Vorotnikov met with deputies (Radio Moscow, May 18, 1989).

41. See the speeches of Yakov Guzbas and Aleksei Boiko to the Congress (Radio Moscow, May 26,1989) as well as the speeches of the deputies named in note 45 below.

42. AP, May 24, 1989.

43. AP, May 23, 1989.

44. *Moscow News*, No. 21, 1989; see also Novosti, May 24, 1989.

45. Vitautas A. Statulevičius and Oleg T. Bogomolov, Radio Moscow, May 26,1989; and Chingiz Aitmatov, Kazimieras A. Antanavičius, and Nursultan A. Nazarbiev, Radio Moscow, May 25, 1989.

46. Radio Moscow, May 24, 1989; AP, May 25, 1989.

47. Vitalii V. Gulii, Radio Moscow, May 27, 1989.

48. *Politicheskoe obrazovanie*, No. 10, 1989, inside front cover.

49. Svyatoslav N. Fedorov, Radio Moscow, May 26, 1989.

50. Gorbachev read the note aloud, Radio Moscow, May 26, 1989.

51. Fedor Burlatsky, Radio Moscow, May 26, 1989.

52. Grigorii A. Posibeev and Vladimir N. Zubkov, Radio Moscow, May 27, 1989.

53. Vladimir A. Zubanov, Radio Moscow, May 26, 1989.

54. See, for example, *Literaturnaya gazeta*, March 8, 1989; interview with Fedor Burlatsky, *Sovetskaya kultura*, April 6, 1989.

55. Vladimir P. Zolotukhin, Radio Moscow, May 26, 1989.

56. Vladimir N. Kudryavtsev, Radio Moscow, May 26, 1989.

57. TASS, April 4, 1989. A detailed breakdown of the composition of the 2,044 who had been elected to the CPD by the end of April appeared in *Izvestia* on May 6, 1989.

58. *Pravda*, April 26, 1989.

59. Central Television, May 27, 1989.

60. *Nedelya*, May 29-June 4, 1989.

61. Ibid.

Figure   The USSR's Legislative & Governmental Bodies

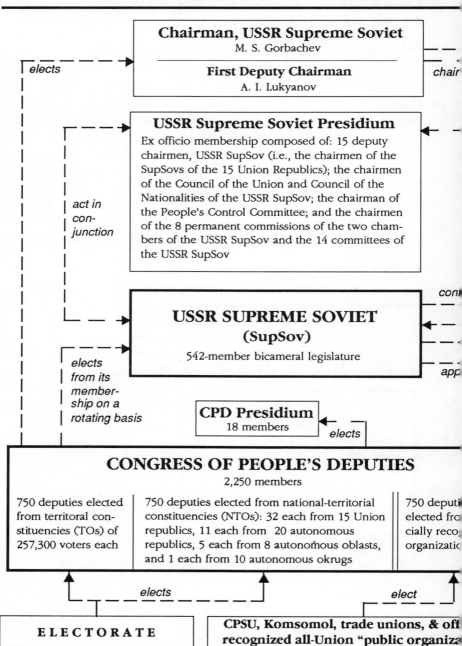

Chairman, USSR Supreme Soviet
M. S. Gorbachev

First Deputy Chairman
A. I. Lukyanov

elects

chair

USSR Supreme Soviet Presidium

Ex officio membership composed of: 15 deputy chairmen, USSR SupSov (i.e., the chairmen of the SupSovs of the 15 Union Republics); the chairmen of the Council of the Union and Council of the Nationalities of the USSR SupSov; the chairman of the People's Control Committee; and the chairmen of the 8 permanent commissions of the two chambers of the USSR SupSov and the 14 committees of the USSR SupSov

act in con- junction

USSR SUPREME SOVIET
(SupSov)

542-member bicameral legislature

con

app

elects from its member- ship on a rotating basis

CPD Presidium
18 members

elects

CONGRESS OF PEOPLE'S DEPUTIES
2,250 members

750 deputies elected from territoral con- stituencies (TOs) of 257,300 voters each

750 deputies elected from national-territorial constituencies (NTOs): 32 each from 15 Union republics, 11 each from 20 autonomous republics, 5 each from 8 autonomous oblasts, and 1 each from 10 autonomous okrugs

750 deputi elected fro cially reco organizatic

elects

elect

ELECTORATE

CPSU, Komsomol, trade unions, & off recognized all-Union "public organiza

Figure   39

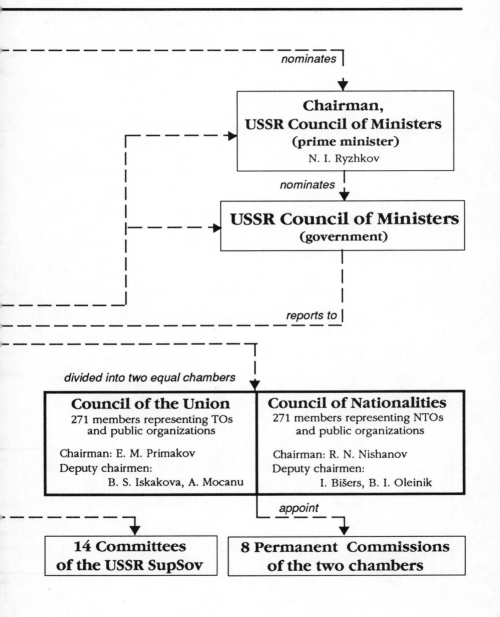

nominates

**Chairman,
USSR Council of Ministers**
(prime minister)
N. I. Ryzhkov

nominates

USSR Council of Ministers
(government)

reports to

divided into two equal chambers

Council of the Union
271 members representing TOs
and public organizations

Chairman: E. M. Primakov
Deputy chairmen:
    B. S. Iskakova, A. Mocanu

Council of Nationalities
271 members representing NTOs
and public organizations

Chairman: R. N. Nishanov
Deputy chairmen:
    I. Bišers, B. I. Oleinik

appoint

**14 Committees
of the USSR SupSov**

**8 Permanent Commissions
of the two chambers**

Part II

BIOGRAPHICAL DIRECTORY OF THE USSR SUPREME SOVIET

1

The Presidium

Chairman, USSR Supreme Soviet

Gorbachev, Mikhail Sergeevich
● General secretary, CPSU CC; chairman, USSR Defense Council. CPSU member. Elected from the CPSU. ● Born March 2, 1931; Russian; graduated from Law Faculty, Moscow State University, 1955. 1970–1978, first secretary, Stavropol Kraikom. Member, CPSU CC since 1971. Achieved national prominence in 1978 when he became CPSU CC secretary for agriculture. Candidate member, Politburo, 1979; member, 1980. Member of USSR SupSov (1984). Appointed Party leader in March 1985; elected chairman, Presidium, USSR SupSov (titular president), September 1988, and to the new post of executive president in May 1989. ● Member, CPD Presidium; chairman, CPD Constitutional Commission; chairman, USSR SupSov.

First Deputy Chairman, USSR Supreme Soviet

Lukyanov, Anatolii Ivanovich
● CPSU member. Elected from the CPSU. ● Born May 7, 1930; Russian; Doctor of Juridical Sciences. Graduated in 1953 from Law Faculty, Moscow State University, where he was a student with Gorbachev and was at one time Gorbachev's superior in the university's Komsomol organization. Displayed himself to be a reformer by writing his dissertation on the "withering away of the state." Extensive experience in administration of USSR SupSov (1969–1976) and in CPSU CC apparatus (1977–1987). Full member, CPSU CC since 1986. 1987–1988, secretary, CPSU CC, and chief, Administrative Organs Department, CPSU CC (supervised military, security, intelligence, and legal institutions). Since 1987, member, Politburo Commission for Further Study of Materials and Documents Related to the Repressions of the Stalin Years. September 1988, appointed candidate member, CPSU CC Politburo and first deputy chairman, Presidium, USSR SupSov (i.e., Gorbachev's deputy); retains a similar position in newly reconstituted SupSov, chairing SupSov sessions whenever Gorbachev is absent. Active in introduction of legal reforms. ● Member, CPD Presidium; member, CPD Drafting Commission;

first deputy chairman, USSR SupSov; chairman, Provisional SupSov Committee for the Struggle against Crime in the USSR.

Deputy Chairmen, USSR Supreme Soviet Presidium

Note: *italicized* names are those of Presidium members who were not elected to the USSR Supreme Soviet. Biographical sketches of all other Presidium members are found in chapters 2 and 3.

Akmatov, Tashtanbek—Chairman, Presidium, Kirgiz SSR SupSov
Astrauskas, Vitautas (Stasevich)—Chairman, Presidium, Lithuanian SSR SupSov
Bazarova, Roza Atamuradovna—Chairman, Presidium, Turkmen SSR SupSov
Cherkezia, Otar Evtikhievich—Chairman, Presidium, Georgian SSR SupSov
Gorbunovs, Anatolijs—Chairman, Presidium, Latvian SSR SupSov
Ibragimov, Mirzaolim Ibragimovich—Chairman, Presidium, Uzbek SSR SupSov
Kafarova, Elmira Mikail kyzy—Chairman, Presidium, Azerbaijan SSR SupSov
Pallaev, Gaibnazar—Chairman, Presidium, Tajik SSR SupSov
Rüütel, Arnold—Chairman, Presidium, Estonian SSR SupSov
Sagdiev, Makhtai Ramazanovich—Chairman, Presidium, Kazakh SSR SupSov
Shevchenko, Valentina Semenovna—Chairman, Presidium, Ukrainian SSR SupSov
Snegur, Mircea (Snegur, Mircha Ivanovich)—Chairman, Presidium, Moldavian SSR SupSov
Tarazevich, Georgii Stanislavovich—Chairman, Presidium, Belorussian SSR SupSov; Chairman, Council of Nationalities Commission on Nationality Policy and Interethnic Relations
Vorotnikov, Vitalii Ivanovich—Chairman, Presidium, RSFSR SupSov
Voskanyan, Grant Mushegovich—Chairman, Presidium, Armenian SSR SupSov

Members, USSR Supreme Soviet Presidium

Aitmatov, Chingiz—Chairman, Council of Nationalities Commission on the Development of Culture, Language, National and Interethnic Traditions, and Preservation of Historical Heritage

Alekseev, Sergei Sergeevich—Chairman, SupSov Committee on Legislation, Legality, and Law and Order

Borodin, Yurii Ivanovich—Chairman, SupSov Committee on Public Health

Bosenko, Nikolai Vasilevich—Chairman, SupSov Committee on Veterans and Invalids

Dzasokhov, Aleksandr Sergeevich—Chairman, SupSov Committee on International Affairs

Eltsin, Boris Nikolaevich—Chairman, SupSov Committee on Construction and Architecture

Foteev, Vladimir Konstantinovich—Chairman, SupSov Committee on *Glasnost*, Rights, and Appeals of Citizens

Gritsenko, Nikolai Nikolaevich—Chairman, Council of the Union Commission on Labor, Prices, and Social Policy

Kiselev, Gennadii Nikolaevich—Chairman, Council of Nationalities Commission on Consumer Goods, Trade, and Communal and Household Services for the Population

Kolbin, Gennadii Vasilevich—Chairman, USSR People's Control Committee

Kucherenko, Viktor Grigorevich—Chairman, Council of the Union Planning and Budgetary Finance Commission

Kurtashin, Vladimir Egorovich—Chairman, Council of the Union Commission on Development of Industry, Energy, Equipment, and Technology

Lapygin, Vladimir Lavrentevich—Chairman, SupSov Committee on Defense and State Security

Matvienko, Valentina Ivanovna—Chairman, SupSov Committee on Women's Affairs, Family Protection, Motherhood, and Childhood

Nishanov, Rafik Nishanovich—Chairman, Council of Nationalities

Pivovarov, Nikolai Dmitrievich—Chairman, SupSov Committee on Soviets of People's Deputies, Development of Government, and Self-Government

Primakov, Evgenii Maksimovich—Chairman, Council of the Union

Ryzhov, Yurii Alekseevich—Chairman, SupSov Committee on Science, Public Education, Culture, and Upbringing

Salykov, Kakimbek—Chairman, SupSov Committee on Ecology and the Rational Use of Natural Resources

Tetenov, Valentin Afanasevich—Chairman, Council of the Union Commission on Transport, Communications, and Information Science

Tsybukh, Valerii Ivanovich—Chairman, SupSov Committee on Youth

Veprev, Arkadii Filimonovich—Chairman, SupSov Committee on Agrarian Questions and Food

Vilkas, Edvardas—Chairman, Council of Nationalities Commission on Social and Economic Development of Union and Autonomous Republics, and Autonomous Oblasts and Okrugs

Vologzhin, Valentin Mikhailovich—Chairman, SupSov Committee on Economic Reform

2

The Council of the Union

Russian Soviet Federated Socialist Republic (RSFSR)

Alekseev, Sergei Sergeevich
● Corresponding member, USSR Academy of Sciences; director, Institute of Philosophy and Law, Urals Department, USSR Academy of Sciences, Sverdlovsk. CPSU member. Elected from the USSR Academy of Sciences.
● Born 1924; legal specialist with higher education; fought in World War II; strong proponent of leasing; for his address to the CPD, see *Sovetskaya kultura*, June 8, 1989; for more on his views see *Pravda*, June 12, 1989, and *Komsomolskaya pravda*, July 11, 1989. ● Member, CPD Constitutional Commission and Constitutional Oversight Commission; member, USSR SupSov Presidium; chairman, SupSov Committee on Legislation, Legality, and Law and Order.

Blaev, Boris Khagutsirovich
● Director, Tungsten-Molybdenum Combine, Tyrnyauz. CPSU member. Elected from TO No. 367, Kabardino-Balkar ASSR. ● Member, Council of the Union Commission on Development of Industry, Energy, and Technology.

Bliznov, Leonid Evgenevich
● Fitter-repairman, Kerchief Production Association, Pavlovsky Posad, Moscow Oblast. CPSU member. Elected from TO No. 38, Moscow Oblast, RSFSR. ● For brief statement, see roundtable discussion, *Moscow News*, May 14, 1989. ● Member, Council of the Union Commission on Development of Industry, Energy, Equipment, and Technology.

Bobyleva, Evdokiya Fedorovna (F)
● Director, secondary school, Odoev, Tula Oblast, RSFSR. CPSU member. Elected from the All-Union Organization of War and Labor Veterans. ● For statement on her concern for rural education and housing for the elderly, see *Sovetskaya Rossiya*, May 5, 1989.
● Member, SupSov Committee on Science, Public Education, Culture, and Upbringing.

Bocharov, Mikhail Aleksandrovich

● Director, Butovsky Construction Materials Combine, Razvilka, Moscow Oblast. CPSU member. Elected from TO No. 23, Moscow.
● Runs his factory on experimental economic principles. For electoral statement calling for expansion of leasing in industry, see *Izvestia*, March 29, 1989. In televised interview, defended striking coal miners, saying their protests showed that the era of "half-baked" measures was over; criticized leading members of newly formed Soviet government for being out of step with "today's requirements" and suggested Gorbachev needed a different team to approach problems in a more "unconventional" and "revolutionary" way (Central Television, July 20, 1989). Opposed economic independence for Baltic republics on grounds it would prejudice economic development in other areas of the USSR (Central Television, July 26, 1989). ● Secretary, SupSov Committee on Construction and Architecture. Founding member, MDG.

Bogdanov, Igor Mikhailovich

● Director, School No. 94, Gorki. CPSU member. Elected from TO No. 156, Gorki Oblast, RSFSR. ● Member, CPD Constitutional Commission; SupSov Committee on Youth.

Bogomolov, Yurii Aleksandrovich

● Director, "Evlashevsky" Sovkhoz, Kuznetsky Raion. CPSU member. Elected from TO No. 254, Penza Oblast, RSFSR. ● Member, SupSov Committee on *Glasnost*, Rights, and Appeals of Citizens.

Borodin, Yurii Ivanovich

● Chairman, Presidium, Siberian Department, USSR Academy of Medical Sciences, Novosibirsk. CPSU member. Elected from USSR Academy of Medical Sciences. ● Was 60 in June 1989. Academic/medical doctor with extensive experience in local government. ● Member, USSR SupSov Presidium; chairman, SupSov Committee on Public Health.

Borovkov, Vyacheslav Aleksandrovich

● Metal worker, "Kirovsky Zavod" Production Association, Leningrad. CPSU member. Elected from the USSR Trade Unions. ● Member, CPD Drafting Commission; SupSov Committee on *Glasnost*, Rights, and Appeals of Citizens.

Burlatsky, Fedor Mikhailovich
● Political observer, *Literaturnaya gazeta*; head, Philosophy Department, Institute of Social Sciences of CPSU CC, Moscow. CPSU member. Elected from the Soviet Peace Foundation. ● Born 1927; Doctor of Philosophy. Prominent journalist and intellectual whose controversial opinions (e.g.,calls for abolition of theater censorship and expansion of small-scale private enterprise) have frequently gotten him into hot water but who has avoided permanently falling afoul of the authorities. Worked under Yurii Andropov in CPSU CC *apparat* in late 1950s. Speech-writer for Khrushchev and Gorbachev. Appointed to post on *Literaturnaya gazeta* following Andropov's rise to power in 1982; under Gorbachev, named to head Public Commission for International Cooperation in Humanitarian Problems and Human Rights. In this capacity, travels frequently to the West and acts as unofficial spokesman of the Gorbachev leadership. Presented draft SupSov appeal to Soviet population in connection with strikes and ethnic unrest, July 25, 1989. ● Member, CPD Constitutional Commission; SupSov Committee on International Affairs.

Chernyaev, Nikolai Fedorovich
● Machine operator, "Krasnoe Znamya" Kolkhoz, Karsunsky Raion. CPSU member. Elected from TO No. 329, Ulyanovsk Oblast, RSFSR. ● Member, SupSov Committee on International Affairs.

Chichik, Yurii Mikhailovich
● Director, "Krasnorechensky" Sovkhoz, Khabarovsk Raion. CPSU member. Elected from TO No. 111, Khabarovsk Krai, RSFSR. ● Member, SupSov Committee on Legislation, Legality, and Law and Order.

Denisov, Anatolii Alekseevich
● Professor, M. I. Kalinin Polytechnic Institute, Leningrad. CPSU member. Elected from TO No. 50, Leningrad. ● See *Pravda*, July 23, 1989 for statement in support of democratic centralism and the leading role of the Party. ● Member, SupSov Committee on Ecology and the Rational Use of Natural Resources.

Dikul, Valentin Ivanovich
● Director, Center for the Rehabilitation of Patients Suffering from Spinal and Brain Injuries and the Consequences of Infantile Cerebral Palsy, Moscow. Elected from TO No. 10, Moscow. ● Calls for expanding

medical rehabilitation centers (*Pravda*, May 13, 1989). ● Member, SupSov Committee on Veterans and Invalids.

Dorokhov, Ivan Vasilevich
● First secretary, Bobrovsky Raikom. CPSU member. Elected from TO No. 153, Voronezh Oblast, RSFSR. ● Member, SupSov Committee on Soviets of People's Deputies, Development of Government, and Self-Government.

Drunina, Yuliya Vladimirovna (F)
● Poet; secretary, USSR Writers' Union Board and RSFSR Writers' Union Board. Elected from the Soviet Women's Committee. ● Electoral platform focused on plight of Afghan veterans and their families (*Pravda*, March 8, 1989).

Druz, Petr Antonovich
● Pensioner, Belovo, Kemerovo Oblast, RSFSR. CPSU member. Elected from the All-Union Organization of War and Labor Veterans. ● Former power station director. Holds ministries responsible for economic distortions for which, he told the CPD, the Party is getting the blame; argues in favor of enterprise independence, leasing, and greater responsibility for local soviets (Central Television, June 7, 1989). ● Member, SupSov Committee on Veterans and Invalids.

Dyakov, Ivan Nikolaevich
● First secretary, Astrakhan Obkom. CPSU member. Elected from TO No. 122, Astrakhan Oblast, RSFSR. ● Born 1937; Russian; higher education in naval engineering and economics. Extensive experience in Party work; former CPSU CC inspector (responsible for Kazakhstan). May 1988, replaced Brezhnevite holdout in current post where he has started cleanup of Astrakhan Party organization. Strong ties to Georgii Razumovsky, a close Gorbachev associate who holds post of CC secretary in charge of personnel. Dyakov received 96.5 percent of the vote in election to the CPD and was one of only a few RSFSR regional Party leaders to be elected to the SupSov; this suggests he is well known outside his own region. ● Member, Council of the Union Commission on Development of Industry, Energy, Equipment, and Technology.

Efimov, Nikolai Vasilevich
● Leader of team of installation workers at the "Stalkonstruktsiya"

Specialized Trust's Construction and Installation Administration, Vyksa. CPSU member. Elected from TO No. 160, Gorki Oblast, RSFSR. ● Member, SupSov Committee on Construction and Architecture.

Egorov, Oleg Mikhailovich
● Second officer, Kaliningrad Refrigeration and Transport Fleet Administration's "Primorsky Bereg" refrigerator ship, Kaliningrad, RSFSR. CPSU member. Elected from the All-Union Komsomol.
● Member, Council of the Union Commission on Transport, Communications, and Information Science.

Emelyanov, Aleksei Mikhailovich
● Department head, Agricultural Economics Faculty, Moscow State University. CPSU member. Elected from TO No. 1, Moscow. ● Strong proponent of economic reform; Eltsin supporter. Election platform stressed need for real cost accounting in agriculture, arguing that contracting and leasing will be ineffectual as long as sovkhozes and kolkhozes continue to be regulated from above (*Ekonomicheskaya gazeta,* No. 10, 1989). Criticized the nomination of CPD deputies by public organizations as being undemocratic (*New Times,* No. 15, 1989). Made forceful speech at CPD on need for democratization and elimination of privilege (*Pravda,* June 9, 1989). ● Member, SupSov Committee on Agrarian Questions and Food.

Ermolaev, Gennadii Mikhailovich
● Director, Mikhailovsky Livestock Breeding Sovkhoz, Kormilovsky Raion. CPSU member. Elected from TO No. 240, Omsk Oblast, RSFSR.
● Member, Council of the Union Commission on Transport, Communications, and Information Science.

Ezhelev, Anatolii Stepanovich
● Chief, *Izvestia*'s Leningrad Correspondent Center. CPSU member. Elected from the USSR Journalists' Union. ● Born 1932; higher education; *Izvestia* feature writer. In 1986 lobbied for democratization of leadership selection in the CPSU; conducted year-long dialogue on the merit of tolerating differing views (*Izvestia,* June 3, 1986). Lauded citizen protests against the razing of Leningrad's historic Hotel "Angleterre" (*Izvestia,* March 27, 1987). ● Member, SupSov Committee on *Glasnost,* Rights, and Appeals of Citizens.

Filshin, Gennadii Innokentevich
● Department chief, Institute of Economics and Organization of Industrial Production, Siberian Department, USSR Academy of Sciences, Irkutsk. CPSU member. Elected from TO No. 171, Irkutsk Oblast, RSFSR. ● Candidate of Economic Sciences. Crusader for development of Siberia through territorial cost accounting and self-financing. Electoral platform called for Siberia to be freed from petty tutelage of ministries (*Sovetskaya Rossiya*, March 24, 1989). ● Member, Council of the Union Planning and Budgetary Finance Commission.

Finogenov, Vladimir Vyacheslavovich
● Polisher, tool shop, "Elektroavtomat" Plant, Alatyr, Chuvash ASSR. CPSU member. Elected from the All-Union Komsomol. ● Member, SupSov Committee on Youth.

Frolov, Konstantin Vasilevich
● Vice president, USSR Academy of Sciences; director, A. Blagonravov Machine Science Institute, USSR Academy of Sciences, Moscow. CPSU member. Elected from the Union of Soviet Societies for Friendship and Cultural Ties with Compatriots Abroad (the Rodina Society). ● Born 1932; Russian; graduated from Bryansk Institute of Transport Machine Building. Member, CPSU CC since 1989. Election platform called for "humanization" of international relations at nongovernmental level (TASS, February 2, 1989). ● Member, SupSov Committee on Science, Public Education, Culture, and Upbringing.

Gamzatov, Rasul Gamzatovich
● Writer. Chairman, Dagestan Writers' Union Board; secretary, RSFSR Writers' Union Board, secretary, USSR Writers' Union Board. CPSU member. Elected from TO No. 365, Dagestan ASSR. ● Born 1923; higher education. Member, Presidium, USSR SupSov (1984). Prolific writer and poet, holder of numerous state awards for his work. In 1973 signed a letter with other writers against Andrei Sakharov (*Pravda*, August 31, 1973). ● Member, SupSov Committee on Legislation, Legality, and Law and Order.

Glazkov, Nikolai Semenovich
● Foreman and team leader, Moscow Decorative Timepiece Plant. CPSU member. Elected from TO No. 18, Moscow. ● Election

platform called for stricter oversight and review of work of industrial ministries (*Vechernyaya Moskva*, May 16, 1989). For statement supporting laws against wage leveling, see *New Times*, No. 15, 1989.
• Member, Council of the Union Commission on Labor, Prices, and Social Policy.

Golik, Yurii Vladimirovich
• Dean of Law Faculty, Kemerovo State University. CPSU member. Elected from TO No. 190, Kemerovo Oblast, RSFSR. • Told the SupSov in July 1989 the miners' strikes were a "scream of despair" at the failure of the CP and official trade unions to protect the rights of workers (TASS, July 24, 1989). • Deputy chairman, CPD Commission to Investigate Materials Linked with the Activity of the USSR Prosecutor's Office Investigation Group Headed by Telman Gdlyan; member, CPD Constitutional Commission; member, CPD Constitutional Oversight Commission; SupSov Committee on Legislation, Legality, and Law and Order.

Golyakov, Aleksandr Ivanovich
• First deputy chairman, All-Union Council of War and Labor Veterans, Moscow. CPSU member. Elected from the All-Union Organization of War and Labor Veterans. • Previously worked in CPSU CC Administrative Organs Department. • Member, CPD Commission to Investigate the April 1989 Events in Tbilisi; SupSov Committee on Veterans and Invalids.

Gorbatko, Viktor Vasilevich
• Major general; chief of faculty, N. E. Zhukovsky Air Force Engineering Academy; chairman, All-Union Society of Philatelists Board, Moscow. Elected from the All-Union Society of Philatelists. • Born 1934; Russian; higher military education. Has served in armed forces since 1953. Twice Hero of the Soviet Union. • Member, Council of the Union Commission on Transport, Communications, and Information Science.

Grachev, Nikolai Petrovich
• Adjuster, Third State Ball Bearing Production Association, Saratov. CPSU member. Elected from TO No. 284, Saratov Oblast, RSFSR.
• Electoral platform called for unconditional independence of enterprises; see *Izvestia*, March 30, 1989. Told Prime Minister Nikolai Ryzhkov at CPD that enterprises should have power to decide how to spend their own profits (Central Television, June 7, 1989). • Member, SupSov

Committee on Soviets of People's Deputies, Development of Government, and Self-Government.

Gritsenko, Nikolai Nikolaevich
● Rector, N. M. Shvernik Higher School of the Trade Union Movement, All-Union Central Council of Trade Unions, Moscow. CPSU member. Elected from the USSR Trade Unions. ● Was 60 in June 1989; Doctor of Economics. For his comments on pressing economic issues, see *Argumenty i fakty*, No. 26, 1989. ● Member, USSR SupSov Presidium; chairman, Council of the Union Commission on Labor, Prices, and Social Policy.

Gross, Viktor Ivanovich
● General director, "Bryansk Automobile Plant" Production Association. CPSU member. Elected from TO No. 129, Bryansk Oblast, RSFSR. ● Member, Council of the Union Planning and Budgetary Finance Commission.

Grudinina, Anna Kornilovna (F)
● Section chief, Borisoglebsk Central Raion Hospital, Voronezh Oblast. Elected from TO No. 151, Voronezh Oblast, RSFSR. ● Member, SupSov Committee on Public Health.

Gubarev, Viktor Andreevich
● Deputy director, "Neftetermmash" Prototype Experimental Machine Building Plant, Chernomorsk, Seversky Raion, Krasnodar Krai. CPSU member. Elected from TO No. 78, Krasnodar Krai, RSFSR. ● Member, Council of the Union Planning and Budgetary Finance Commission.

Gudilina, Valentina Grigorevna (F)
● Department chief, Solnechnogorsk Central Raion Hospital. Elected from TO No. 42, Moscow Oblast, RSFSR.

Gutskalov, Nikolai Ivanovich
● Captain-director of Murmansk Trawler Fleet Administration's large autonomous trawler "Marshal Eremenko," Murmansk, RSFSR. CPSU member. Elected from the USSR Trade Unions. ● Member, Council of the Union Commission on Transport, Communications, and Information Science.

Iovlev, Dmitrii Mikhailovich
- Metalworker, "Leninist Komsomol" Automobile Plant, "Moskvich" Production Association, Moscow. CPSU member. Elected from the CPSU.
- Born 1921. Election program focused on need for restoration of order; argued that economic planning should be precise and suppliers be given compulsory, taut contracts (*Pravda*, January 30, 1989). ● Member, SupSov Committee on *Glasnost*, Rights, and Appeals of Citizens.

Ivanov, Kliment Egorovich
- General director, "Sever" Agrocombine, Yakutsk. CPSU member. Elected from TO No. 402, Yakut ASSR. ● Member, Council of the Union Planning and Budgetary Finance Commission.

Ivchenko, Ivan Mikhailovich
- Link leader, "Oktyabr" Kolkhoz, Chertkovsky Raion, Rostov Oblast. CPSU member. Elected from TO No. 273, Rostov Oblast, RSFSR.

Kalmykov, Yurii Khamzatovich
- Chief of department, D. I. Kursky Law Institute, Saratov. CPSU member. Elected from TO No. 283, Saratov Oblast, RSFSR. ● In official capacity on the Legislation Committee, playing a particularly active role in the introduction of new Soviet legislation. ● Member, CPD Constitutional Commission; CPD Constitutional Oversight Commission; deputy chairman, SupSov Committee on Legislation. Legality, and Law and Order.

Kasyan, Vladimir Vasilevich
- Section chief, "Pervomaisky" Sovkhoz, Anapsky Raion. CPSU member. Elected from TO No. 81, Krasnodar Krai, RSFSR. ● Member, SupSov Committee on Soviets of People's Deputies, Development of Government, and Self-Government.

Kazachenko, Petr Petrovich
- Chairman, "Voskhod" Kolkhoz, Uzlovsky Raion. CPSU member. Elected from TO No. 317, Tula Oblast, RSFSR. ● Member, Council of the Union Planning and Budgetary Finance Commission. Member MDG.

Kazarin, Aleksei Aleksandrovich
- Carpenter and concrete worker, "Sharyadrev" Timber Processing Production Association, Kostroma Oblast, RSFSR. CPSU member. Elected from the All-Union Komsomol. ● Member, SupSov Committee on Youth.

Khadzhiev, Salambek Naibovich
● General director, "Grozneftekhim" Scientific Production Association, Groznyi. CPSU member. Elected from TO No. 396, Chechen-Ingush ASSR. ● Expressed disappointment at the CPD's failure to establish efficient operating procedures, its intolerance of divergent opinions, and its tendency to dictate to people from above (*Izvestia*, June 12, 1989).
● Member, Council of the Union Planning and Budgetary Finance Commission.

Khmura, Valerii Vasilevich
● Chairman, Olginsky Rural Ispolkom, Primorsko-Akhtarsky Raion. CPSU member. Elected from TO No. 84, Krasnodar Krai, RSFSR. ● Spoke at CPD on need to enhance authority of village and settlement soviets; also addressed economic problems of rural areas and ecological issues in the Kuban and the Aral Sea area (*Pravda*, June 4, 1989). ● Member, SupSov Committee on Soviets of People's Deputies, Development of Government, and Self-Government.

Kim En Un
● Senior scientific associate, Omsk State University. CPSU member. Elected from TO No. 238, Omsk Oblast, RSFSR. ● Member, SupSov Committee on International Affairs. Member, MDG.

Kisin, Viktor Ivanovich
● Chief, New Technology Administration, I. A. Likhachev Automobile Plant ("ZIL"), Moscow. CPSU member. Elected from the All-Union "Znanie" Society. ● Electoral platform pledged to make SupSov an active body rather than the rubber stamp of the past (*Pravda*, March 6, 1989). Interviewed on Soviet television in connection with new law on property, expressed strong support for wide range of different forms of property for the USSR (Central Television, August 9, 1989).
● Deputy chairman, Council of the Union Commission on Development of Industry, Energy, Equipment, and Technology. Member, MDG.

Klimov, Mikhail Valerevich
● Deputy chief physician, Vyshnii Volochek Central Raion Hospital, Elected from TO No. 183, Kalinin Oblast, RSFSR. ● Member, SupSov Committee on Women's Affairs, Family Protection, Motherhood, and Childhood.

Konkov, Pavel Ivanovich
● Pensioner, Krasnoyarsk, RSFSR. CPSU member. Elected from the All-Union Organization of War and Labor Veterans. ● Member, SupSov Committee on Veterans and Invalids.

Kopylova, Aleksandra Vasilevna (F)
● Chief, Public Education Department, Mtsensk Gorispolkom. CPSU member. Elected from TO No. 250, Orel Oblast, RSFSR. ● Member, SupSov Committee on Science, Public Education, Culture, and Upbringing.

Kopysov, Nikolai Mikhailovich
● Controller, radio plant, Izhevsk. CPSU member. Elected from TO No. 392, Udmurt ASSR. ● Member, Council of the Union Commission on Transport, Communications, and Information Science.

Korenev, Aleksandr Anatolevich
● Leader of a team of drivers, No. 1 Motor Transport Production Association, Kurgan, RSFSR. CPSU member. Elected from the USSR Trade Unions. ● Member, Council of the Union Commission on Transport, Communications, and Information Science.

Koryugin, Nikolai Nikolaevich
● Chief, Economic Research Laboratory, "Fiftieth Anniversary of the USSR" Metallurgical Combine, Cherepovets. CPSU member. Elected from TO No. 148, Vologda Oblast, RSFSR. ● Was 38 in April 1989. For brief profile, see *Izvestia*, April 13, 1989. ● Member, SupSov Committee on Economic Reform.

Krasnokutsky, Boris Ivanovich
● Chairman, Ya. M. Sverdlov Kolkhoz, Sysertsky Raion. CPSU member. Elected from TO No. 298, Sverdlovsk Oblast, RSFSR. ● Member, SupSov Committee on Agrarian Questions and Food.

Kryuchenkova, Nadezhda Aleksandrovna (F)
● Teacher, Secondary School No. 2, Inzhavino Workers' Settlement. CPSU member. Elected from TO No. 309, Tambov Oblast, RSFSR. ● Member, CPD Drafting Commission; SupSov Committee on Science, Public Education, Culture, and Upbringing.

Kulikov, Viktor Georgievich
● Marshal of the Soviet Union; general inspector, USSR Ministry of Defense. CPSU member. Elected from the All-Union Organization of War and Labor Veterans. ● Born July 5, 1921; Russian; graduated from Frunze Military Academy (1953) and Military Academy of the General Staff (1959). Veteran of World War II; wounded six times. Rose through the military by virtue of his performance in the war and in military service abroad. 1969–1971, commander in chief, Group of Soviet Troops in Germany. 1971–1977, chief of General Staff, USSR Armed Forces; 1971–1989, USSR first deputy minister of defense. Protégé of former Soviet defense minister Andrei Grechko. With Sergei Akhromeev, one of the last two remaining Soviet marshals. Member of USSR SupSov (1984). Member, CPSU CC, 1971–1989 (one of 110 "dead souls" retired in April 1989). ● Member, SupSov Committee on Veterans and Invalids.

Kurtashin, Vladimir Egorovich
● General director, "Kriogenmash" Scientific Production Association, Balashikha, Moscow Oblast, RSFSR. CPSU member. Elected from the USSR Trade Unions. ● Was 57 in June 1989. ● Member, USSR SupSov Presidium; chairman, Council of the Union Commission on Development of Industry, Energy, Equipment, and Technology.

Kuzovlev, Anatolii Tikhonovich
● Chairman, Kalinin Kolkhoz, Kanevsky Raion, Krasnodar Krai, RSFSR. CPSU member. Elected from the Council of Kolkhozes. ● Member, SupSov Committee on Agrarian Questions and Food.

Laptev, Ivan Dmitrievich
● Chief editor, *Izvestia*, Moscow. CPSU member. Elected from the CPSU. ● Born 1934; Russian; graduated from the Siberian Highways Institute and Academy of Social Sciences of CPSU CC. Doctor of Philosophy. 1973–1978, consultant, Propaganda Department, CPSU CC. 1982, deputy chief editor of *Pravda*. Appointed to current position in June 1984. Under his editorship, *Izvestia* has become a flagship of economic and political reform. Candidate member, CPSU CC, since 1986. Reportedly refused to publish the Andreeva letter (1988). Described by *The Guardian* (December 15, 1987) as "a committed reformer who knows the limits of *glasnost*." ● Member, CPD Constitutional Commission; CPD Drafting Commission; SupSov Committee on International Affairs.

Leonchev, Vladimir Aleksandrovich
● Leader of a metalworking team, "Fiftieth Anniversary of the USSR" Petrochemical Combine, Novokuibyshevsk. CPSU member. Elected from TO No. 208, Kuibyshev Oblast, RSFSR. ● Expressed concern about the construction of plant for destroying chemical weapons near Chapaevsk, Kuibyshev Oblast, on grounds it would jeopardize the welfare of local inhabitants and cause ecological damage (Central Television, June 2, 1989). ● Member, SupSov Committee on Ecology and the Rational Use of Natural Resources.

Lubenchenko, Konstantin Dmitrievich
● Senior lecturer, Law Faculty, Moscow State University. CPSU member. Elected from TO No. 40, Moscow Oblast, RSFSR. ● Member, CPD Commission to Investigate Materials Linked with the Activity of the USSR Prosecutor's Office Investigation Group Headed by Telman Gdlyan; SupSov Committee on Legislation, Legality, and Law and Order. Member, MDG.

Lunev, Viktor Andreevich
● Lathe operator, "Kompressor" Refrigeration Machine Building Plant, Moscow. CPSU member. Elected from the CPSU. ● Born 1949. Worker-hero; numerous labor awards (*Pravda*, March 26, 1989). ● Member, Council of the Union Commission on Labor, Prices, and Social Policy.

Lushnikov, Vladimir Petrovich
● Drifter, "Intaugol" Production Association's "Vostochnaya" Coal Mine, Inta. CPSU member. Elected from TO No. 372, Komi ASSR. ● Met with striking coal miners from Pechora Basin and presented their appeal to SupSov session (Central Television, July 24, 1989). ● Member, Council of the Union Commission on Labor, Prices, and Social Policy.

Maiboroda, Viktor Alekseevich
● Cutter-polisher, freight car building plant, Ust-Katav. Elected from TO No. 340, Chelyabinsk Oblast, RSFSR. ● Member, SupSov Committee on *Glasnost*, Rights, and Appeals of Citizens.

Malkova, Evgeniya Kirillovna (F)
● Foreman, Workshop No. 5, Clothing Production and Repair Factory No. 1, "Siluet" Production Association, Moscow. CPSU member. Elected from the USSR Trade Unions. ● Member, Council of the Union Commission on Labor, Prices, and Social Policy.

Maltsev, Innokentii Ivanovich
● Planer, Efremov "Krasnyi Proletarii" Machine Tool Manufacturing Plant, Moscow. CPSU member. Elected from the All-Union Organization of War and Labor Veterans. ● Member, Council of the Union Commission on Labor, Prices, and Social Policy.

Manaenkov, Yurii Alekseevich
● Secretary, CPSU CC. CPSU member. Elected from TO No. 222, Lipetsk Oblast, RSFSR. ● Born August 2, 1936; Russian; higher agricultural and Party education. Experience in journalism and agriculture. Member, CPSU CC since 1986. First secretary, Lipetsk Obkom, 1984-1989. Praised by *Pravda* (August 11, 1986) for cleaning up corruption in Lipetsk; orchestrated a personnel shake-up involving 645 persons in two and a half years (*Partiinaya zhizn*, May 1988). Lauded in *Krasnaya zvezda* (June 14, 1987) for preparation of youth for military service. For statement in support of "responsible" *glasnost*, see *Sovetskaya kultura*, May 9, 1988. Member of USSR SupSov (1984). Made conservative speech at meeting of regional Party leaders (July 18, 1989), arguing that CPSU must increase attention to cadre selection and strengthen role as political vanguard of Soviet people (*Pravda*, July 21, 1989). ● Member, SupSov Committee on Agrarian Questions and Food.

Markov, Oleg Ivanovich
● Arc welder, "Sibenergomash" Production Association, Barnaul. CPSU member. Elected from TO No. 65, Altai Krai, RSFSR. ● Member, Council of the Union Commission on Development of Industry, Energy, Equipment, and Technology.

Matvienko, Valentina Ivanovna (F)
● Deputy chairman, Leningrad Gorispolkom. CPSU member. Elected from the Soviet Women's Committee. ● Was 40 in June 1989. Former Chairman, Leningrad Obkom Komsomol, and member, Komsomol CC Buro. ● Member, USSR SupSov Presidium; chairman, SupSov Committee on Women's Affairs, Family Protection, Motherhood, and Childhood.

Medikov, Viktor Yakovlevich
● Prorector, Siberian Metallurgical Institute, Novokuznetsk. CPSU member. Elected from TO No. 195, Kemerovo Oblast, RSFSR. ● Candidate of Economic Sciences. Entered public eye during July 1989 miners' strike when acted as intermediary between SupSov and strikers from his native

Kuznetsk Basin. Supported strikers, who, he said, worked hard for few benefits, but called on them to return to work (Central Television, July 17, 1989). ● Deputy chairman, SupSov Special Commission on Problems of Soviet Germans; member, CPD Mandate Commission; member, SupSov Committee on Economic Reform. Member, MDG.

Medvedev, Roy Aleksandrovich
● Historian, Moscow. CPSU member. Elected from TO No. 6, Moscow.
● Born November 14, 1925; Russian; son of Marxist philosopher who perished in the Great Purge of 1938. Studied philosophy at Leningrad State University and received graduate degree in pedagogical sciences. Emerged as leading anti-Stalinist scholar after the Twentieth and Twenty-second Party Congresses (1956 and 1961). Prolific writer; editor, 1964–1971, of influential *samizdat* publication, *Politichesky dnevnik* (Political Diary). Expelled from CP in 1969 after his anti-Stalinist work, *Let History Judge*, was published in the West; continued private research on historical themes, frequently publishing his work in *samizdat* and abroad. Has advocated ideological diversity to allow the USSR to draw on Western models of social democracy (*Leninism and Western Socialism*, 1981). Restored to official favor under Gorbachev; readmitted to CPSU in April 1989 after winning seat in CPD. His works are now widely excerpted in the Soviet press, and Soviet editions of previously banned books are in preparation. Medvedev is among the mainstream reformers supporting Gorbachev's program, arguing that evolutionary political change, guided "from above" by the Party, is the most viable approach. Denies the need for a multiparty system, suggesting the People's Control Committee might serve as the functional equivalent of an opposition party (*Izvestia*, June 9, 1989). Concerning MDG, Medvedev told *L' Unità* (August 10, 1989) that he was not against the idea of an opposition group in the CPD "as long as it does not threaten our still fragile democracy." ● Chairman, CPD Commission to Investigate Materials Linked with the Activity of the USSR Prosecutor's Office Investigation Group Headed by Telman Gdlyan; chairman, CPD Drafting Commission; member, SupSov Committee on Legislation, Legality, and Law and Order.

Menshatov, Aleksei Dmitrievich
● Director, "Azinsky" State Pedigree Stud Farm, Chernushinsky Raion. CPSU member. Elected from TO No. 262, Perm Oblast, RSFSR.
● Member, SupSov Committee on Agrarian Questions and Food.

Mikhedov, Fedor Fedorovich
● Leader of a team of drift miners, "Tsentralnaya" Coal Mine, "Primorskugol" Production Association, Partizansk. CPSU member. Elected from TO No. 100, Primorsky Krai, RSFSR. ● Member, Council of the Union Commission on Development of Industry, Energy, Equipment, and Technology.

Militenko, Svetlana Aleksandrovna (F)
● Department head, "Lesnaya polyana" Sanatorium, Pyatigorsk. CPSU member. Elected from TO No. 109, Stavropol Krai, RSFSR. ● Member, SupSov Committee on Ecology and the Rational Use of Natural Resources.

Minin, Viktor Mikhailovich
● Chief, mechanical shop, Glebovskoe Poultry Production Association, Kholshcheviki Settlement, Istrinsky Raion, Moscow Oblast, RSFSR. CPSU member. Elected from the All-Union Komsomol. ● In pre-CPD interview called for a law on youth (*Pravda*, May 25, 1989). ● Member, CPD Drafting Commission; SupSov Committee on Youth.

Mukhametzyanov, Aklim Kasimovich
● General director, "Tatneft" Production Association, Almetevsk. CPSU member. Elected from TO No. 386, Tatar ASSR. ● Born 1930; Tatar; graduated from Moscow Institute of Petrochemical and Gas Industry. Has worked in petroleum industry for 40 years. Member of USSR SupSov (1984). ● Member, SupSov Committee on International Affairs.

Naumov, Sergei Yakovlevich
● Chairman, "Marksist" Kolkhoz, Baigazina, Argayashsky Raion. CPSU member. Elected from TO No. 338, Chelyabinsk Oblast, RSFSR. ● Campaigned in elections against the construction of three breeder reactors in his region, defeating the chief of construction for the Kyshtym nuclear waste disposal complex (*Sovetskaya Rossiya*, March 3, 1989). ● Member, SupSov Committee on Soviets of People's Deputies, Development of Government, and Self-Government.

Neelov, Yurii Vasilevich
● Chairman, Surgut Raiispolkom. CPSU member. Elected from TO No. 325, Tyumen Oblast, RSFSR. ● Member, Council of the Union Commission on Transport, Communications, and Information Science.

Neumyvakin, Aleksandr Yakovlevich
● Chairman, Central Board, All-Russian Society for the Blind, Moscow. CPSU member. Elected from the Soviet Charity and Health Foundation.
● Blind since age 33; has worked in current post for 15 years. For view on the importance of charity (a subject never mentioned in the official Soviet press until Gorbachev's rise to power), see *Moskovskie novosti,* No. 22, 1987. ● Member, SupSov Committee on Veterans and Invalids.

Nikanorov, Igor Alekseevich
● Lathe operator, Machine Tool Plant, Ryazan, RSFSR. CPSU member. Elected from the All-Union Komsomol. ● Born 1958; Russian. Member of USSR SupSov (1984). ● Member, SupSov Committee on International Affairs.

Nikolsky, Boris Nikolaevich
● Chief editor, journal *Neva,* Leningrad. CPSU member. Elected from TO No. 58, Leningrad. ● Born 1931; higher education in literature. Election platform advocated a multiparty system and lauded new atmosphere in journalism in which editors no longer have to answer to "someone standing behind them" (Radio Moscow, March 9, 1988). In speech to CPD, said *glasnost* needs to be deepened and legally protected (*Izvestia,* June 5, 1989); also proposed formation of commission to investigate how USSR became militarily involved in Afghanistan (Central Television, June 9, 1989). ● Member, SupSov Committee on *Glasnost,* Rights, and Appeals of Citizens.

Nuzhnyi, Vladimir Pavlovich
● Lease collective leader, "Rossiya" Kolkhoz and Breeding Plant, Apanasenkovsky Raion. CPSU member. Elected from TO No. 105, Stavropol Krai, RSFSR. ● Member, SupSov Committee on Economic Reform.

Orekhov, Anatolii Pavlovich
● Chairman, Raiispolkom, Karymskoe Settlement. CPSU member. Elected from TO No. 343, Chita Oblast, RSFSR. ● Defeated Chita Obkom first secretary, CPSU CC member Nikolai Malkov, in CPD elections. Advocates extensive introduction of leasing and family cooperatives (*Sovetskaya Rossiya,* April 8, 1989). ● Member, SupSov Committee on Soviets of People's Deputies, Development of Government, and Self-Government.

Ostroukhov, Viktor Alekseevich
● Secretary, Party Committee, "Sibkabel" Production Association, Tomsk, RSFSR. CPSU member. Elected from the CPSU. ● Born 1939.
● Member, Council of the Union Commission on Development of Industry, Energy, Equipment, and Technology.

Pamfilova, Ella Aleksandrovna (F)
● Chairman, Trade Union Committee, Central Mechanical Repair Plant, "Mosenergo" Production Association, Moscow. CPSU member. Elected from the USSR Trade Unions. ● Member, CPD Mandate Commission; SupSov Committee on Ecology and the Rational Use of Natural Resources.

Panteleev, Nikolai Vasilevich
● Lathe operator, Lepse Electrical Machine Building Plant, Kirov, RSFSR. CPSU member. Elected from the USSR Trade Unions. ● Member, Council of the Union Commission on Labor, Prices, and Social Policy.

Penyagin, Aleksandr Nikolaevich
● Refractory materials maker, electrometallurgy combine, Chelyabinsk. CPSU candidate member. Elected from TO No. 333, Chelyabinsk Oblast, RSFSR. ● Member, SupSov Committee on Ecology and the Rational Use of Natural Resources.

Piryazeva, Nina Mikhailovna (F)
● Electrical assembly worker, "Sibselmash" Production Association, Novosibirsk. Elected from TO No. 229, Novosibirsk Oblast, RSFSR.
● Born 1941; Russian. Has held current position since 1962. Complained the RSFSR was acting too slowly in adopting a plan for self-financing (TASS, July 28, 1989). Member of RSFSR SupSov. ● Member, Council of the Union Commission on Development of Industry, Energy, Equipment, and Technology.

Pivovarov, Nikolai Dmitrievich
● Chairman, Rostov-na-Donu Oblispolkom. CPSU member. Elected from TO No. 272, Rostov Oblast, RSFSR. ● Born 1931; Russian; graduated from Novocherkassk Polytechnical Institute and Higher Party School. Extensive experience in local government and Party organs. Member of RSFSR SupSov. For statement on work of his SupSov committee, see *Izvestia*, July 15, 1989. ● Member, CPD Drafting Commission; member,

USSR SupSov Presidium; chairman, SupSov Committee on Soviets of People's Deputies, Development of Government, and Self-Government.

Pokhodnya, Grigorii Semenovich
● Shop chief, Frunze Kolkhoz, Belgorodsky Raion, Belgorod Oblast, RSFSR. Elected from the CPSU. ● Born 1949. ● Member, SupSov Committee on Agrarian Questions and Food.

Postnikov, Viktor Ivanovich
● General director, "Stavropolskoe" Broiler Production Association, Stavropol, RSFSR. CPSU member. Elected from the CPSU. ● Born 1924; Russian; graduated from Higher Party School. Extensive experience in local government and Party organs. Has worked in current post since 1974. Heads first agricultural enterprise in the Northern Caucasus to operate on cost accounting basis; credited with pioneering new methods of management now being applied nationwide. Postnikov's innovations were supported by the then Stavropol Kraikom first secretary, Mikhail Gorbachev (TASS, August 2, 1988). Created stir at Nineteenth CPSU Conference when he criticized Gorbachev for being too lenient with bureaucrats (Central Television, June 29, 1988). In same speech, called for price reform and enterprise independence, saying it was useless to free enterprises from ministerial tutelage and then subordinate them to the soviets. Hero of Socialist Labor. Member of RSFSR SupSov.
● Member, SupSov Committee on Economic Reform.

Pribylova, Nadezhda Nikolaevna (F)
● Department head; professor, Kursk Medical Institute, RSFSR. CPSU member. Elected from the Soviet Women's Committee. ● Member, SupSov Committee on Public Health.

Primakov, Evgenii Maksimovich
● CPSU member. Elected from the CPSU. ● Born October 29, 1929; Russian; Doctor of Economics. Author of numerous books and articles on international relations, arms control, and the Middle East; one of the principal architects of Gorbachev's "new thinking." 1985–1989, director, Institute of World Economics and International Relations (IMEMO), USSR Academy of Sciences. Since 1988, member, Commission on International Policy, CPSU CC. Participated in all four Reagan-Gorbachev summits. Member, CPSU CC since 1989. Elected to current post in June 1989. Considered a liberal reformer. Attended founding meeting of MDG

but declined to join the group, calling on radical deputies to work in SupSov committees rather than form a separate parliamentary coalition (Reuters, July 27, 1989). ● Member, CPD Constitutional Commission; CPD Drafting Commission. Member, USSR SupSov Presidium; chairman, Council of the Union, USSR SupSov; chairman, USSR SupSov Commission for the Examination of Privileges Enjoyed by Certain Categories of Citizens.

Pukhova, Zoya Pavlovna (F)

● Chairman, Soviet Women's Committee, Moscow. CPSU member. Elected from the Soviet Women's Committee. ● Born 1936; Russian; higher education. Achieved fame in 1970s when Soviet press claimed the weaving mill she then headed achieved the highest labor productivity in the world textile industry. Appointed chairman, Ivanovo Oblispolkom in 1985. Much lauded in the "era of stagnation" for her labor achievements (see, for example, *Izvestia*, January 2, 1982). Hero of Socialist Labor. Member of USSR SupSov (1984). Appointed to her current post in 1987. Delivered hard-hitting speech in defense of women's rights at Nineteenth Party Conference (*Pravda*, July 2, 1988). ● Member, CPD Constitutional Commission; SupSov Committee on Women's Affairs, Family Protection, Motherhood, and Childhood.

Rakhimov, Murtaza Gubaidullovich

● Director, "Twenty-second CPSU Congress" Oil Refinery, Ufa. CPSU member. Elected from TO No. 351, Bashkir ASSR. ● Member, CPD Drafting Commission; Council of the Union Commission on Development of Industry, Energy, Equipment, and Technology.

Rakhmanova, Marina Nikolaevna (F)

● Department head, Orenburg Medical Institute, Orenburg, RSFSR. CPSU member. Elected from the V. I. Lenin Soviet Children's Foundation. ● Member, SupSov Committee on Women's Affairs, Family Protection, Motherhood, and Childhood.

Reshetnikov, Anatolii Vasilevich

● Deputy shop chief, Kaluga Engine Building Production Association. Elected from TO No. 185, Kaluga Oblast, RSFSR. ● Member, Council of the Union Commission on Development of Industry, Energy, Equipment, and Technology. Member, MDG: sees it as a "motor inside the collective of People's Deputies" (Radio Moscow, July 30, 1989).

Rogatin, Boris Nikolaevich
● Chairman, Voluntary Physical Education and Sports Society, All-Union Central Council, AUCCTU, Moscow. CPSU member. Elected from USSR Public Sports Organizations. ● Member, SupSov Committee on Public Health.

Rogozhina, Vera Aleksandrovna (F)
● Senior scientific associate, Institute of the Earth's Core, Siberian Department, USSR Academy of Sciences, Irkutsk, RSFSR. CPSU member. Elected from the Soviet Women's Committee. ● Member, Council of the Union Commission on Labor, Prices, and Social Policy.

Ryumin, Valerii Viktorovich
● Deputy chief designer, "Energiya" Scientific Production Organization, Moscow. CPSU member. Elected from the CPSU. ● Born 1939. ● Member, SupSov Committee on Defense and State Security.

Ryzhov, Yurii Alekseevich
● Rector, Sergo Ordzhonikidze Aviation Institute, Moscow. CPSU member. Elected from TO No. 14, Moscow. ● Was 59 in June 1989. Doctor of Technical Sciences. Has worked in same institute for almost 30 years, rising from lecturer to rector. For article entitled "Science and Morality Are Indivisible," see *Izvestia*, July 17, 1989. ● Member, USSR SupSov Presidium; chairman, SupSov Committee on Science, Public Education, Culture, and Upbringing.

Sapegin, Aleksei Andreevich
● Electric locomotive engineer, Smolensk Locomotive Depot of the Belorussian Railroad. CPSU member. Elected from TO No. 305, Smolensk Oblast, RSFSR. ● Member, Council of the Union Commission on Transport, Communications, and Information Science.

Sarakaev, Archil Totrazovich
● Chairman, Kalinin Kolkhoz, Irafsky Raion. CPSU member. Elected from TO No. 380, North Ossetian ASSR. ● Member, Council of the Union Planning and Budgetary Finance Commission.

Savitskaya, Svetlana Evgenevna (F)
● Test pilot and cosmonaut; deputy department head, "Energiya" Scientific Production Association, Moscow. CPSU member. Elected from

the Soviet Peace Foundation. ● Born August 8, 1948; graduated from Moscow Aviation Institute. A parachutist and former test pilot who has set 18 flying records; USSR's second female cosmonaut and the first woman ever to walk in space. Vice president of Soviet Peace Foundation. For interview defending budget allocations for Soviet space program, see *Ekonomicheskaya gazeta*, June 3, 1989.

Savostyuk, Oleg Mikhailovich
● Graphic artist; secretary, USSR Artists' Union Board; chairman, Moscow Organization of the RSFSR Artists' Union Board. CPSU member. Elected from the USSR Artists' Union. ● Member, SupSov Committee on *Glasnost*, Rights, and Appeals of Citizens.

Sazonov, Nikolai Semenovich
● Secretary, Party committee, Automatic Lathe Unit, Kama Truck Plant, Naberezhnye Chelny. Elected from TO No. 384, Tatar ASSR. ● Member, SupSov Committee on Economic Reform.

Shaidulin, Midkhat Idiyatovich
● Pensioner, Ufa, Bashkir ASSR. CPSU member. Elected from the All-Union Organization of War and Labor Veterans. ● Member, SupSov Committee on Veterans and Invalids.

Sharin, Leonid Vasilevich
● First secretary, Amur Obkom, Blagoveshchensk. CPSU member. Elected from TO No. 116, Amur Oblast, RSFSR. ● Born 1934; Russian; graduate of Vladivostok Higher Naval Academy and Higher Party School. Member, CPSU CC since 1986. 1979–1983, first secretary, Vladivostok Gorkom; 1984–1985, CPSU CC inspector; named to current post, June 1985. One of the few RSFSR obkom first secretaries elected to the USSR SupSov; one of a number of officials who rose to prominence from the Vladivostok City Party organization of the late 1970s and early 1980s. ● Member, SupSov Committee on Defense and State Security.

Shashkov, Nikolai Vladimirovich
● Manager, Nikitinskoe Department of the "Vasilevsky" Sovkhoz, Shuisky Raion. Elected from TO No. 169, Ivanovo Oblast, RSFSR. ● Strong proponent of agricultural leasing who declared his commitment to work for the regeneration of rural Russia (APN, May 25, 1989). ● Member, SupSov Committee on Agrarian Questions and Food.

Shekhovtsov, Viktor Afanasevich
● Deputy dean, Law Faculty, Far Eastern State University, Vladivostok. Elected from TO No. 97, Maritime Krai, RSFSR. ● In electoral platform promised to draw attention of CPD to local issues (*Izvestia*, March 30, 1989). ● Member, SupSov Committee on Soviets of People's Deputies, Development of Government, and Self-Government.

Shishov, Viktor Aleksandrovich
● Director, "Vazhsky" Sovkhoz, Blagoveshchenskoe, Velsky Raion. CPSU member. Elected from TO No. 119, Arkhangelsk Oblast, RSFSR. ● Member, Council of the Union Planning and Budgetary Finance Commission.

Shmal, Yurii Yakovlevich
● Director, Maslyaninsky Sovkhoz, Novosibirsk Oblast. CPSU member. Elected from TO No. 235, RSFSR.

Shtepo, Viktor Ivanovich
● Director general, Volgograd "Volga-Don" Specialized Production Association, Bereslavka Settlement, Kalachevsky Raion, Volgograd Oblast, RSFSR. CPSU member. Elected from the CPSU. ● Born 1928; for favorable feature article on his managerial skills, see *Ekonomicheskaya gazeta*, No. 8, 1989. ● Member, SupSov Committee on Agrarian Questions and Food.

Shukshin, Anatolii Stepanovich
● Grinder, Far East Power Machine-Building Plant, Khabarovsk, RSFSR. CPSU member. Elected from the CPSU. ● Born 1947. Electoral platform called for intensive development of Soviet Far East (*Sovetskaya Rossiya*, January 26, 1989). ● Member, SupSov Committee on Veterans and Invalids.

Skvortsov, Vladimir Vitalevich
● Shop chief, Motor Vehicle Lighting Equipment Plant, Vyazniki. CPSU member. Elected from TO No. 135, Vladimir Oblast, RSFSR. ● Member, Council of the Union Commission on Labor, Prices, and Social Policy.

Sleptsov, Sergei Efimovich
● Machine operator, "Churovichsky" Sovkhoz, Klimovsky Raion, Bryansk Oblast, RSFSR. Elected from the All-Union Komsomol. ● Member, Council of the Union Commission on Labor, Prices, and Social Policy.

Smorodin, Ivan Mikhailovich
● Controller, "Volna" Production Association, Novgorod. Elected from
TO No. 227, Novgorod Oblast, RSFSR. ● Member, SupSov Committee on
Economic Reform.

Sobchak, Anatolii Aleksandrovich
● Head, Law Faculty, Leningrad State University. CPSU member. Elected
from TO No. 47, Leningrad. ● Emerged as one of the most radical anti-
establishment spokesmen in the CPD and SupSov. Harshly critical of
the Tbilisi massacre (*Narodnoe obrazovanie*, July 12, 1989); argued that
officials of top political bodies such as the Politburo should not serve
on the committee overseeing the KGB (*Izvestia*, July 15, 1989); called
SupSov's endorsement of Baltic economic autonomy a "half measure"
(*Washington Post*, July 30, 1989). ● Chairman, CPD Commission to
Investigate the April 1989 Events in Tbilisi. Member, CPD Constitutional
Commission; CPD Constitutional Oversight Commission; SupSov
Committee on Legislation, Legality and Law and Order. Founding
member, MDG.

Sokolova, Yuliya Yurevna (F)
● Senior instructor, Soviet Army and Navy Main Political Directorate,
Moscow. CPSU member. Elected from the Soviet Women's Committee.
● Born 1932; Russian; graduate of Leningrad State Pedagogical Institute.
Has held various teaching positions in the armed forces since 1958.
● Member, SupSov Committee on *Glasnost*, Rights, and Appeals of
Citizens.

Sotnikov, Nikolai Ivanovich
● Director, Leningrad Ceramics Plant. CPSU member. Elected from TO
No. 60, Leningrad Oblast, RSFSR. ● Member, SupSov Committee on
Construction and Architecture.

Stadnik, Vladimir Yakovlevich
● Workshop chief, Machine Building Plant, Lukhovitsy. CPSU member.
Elected from TO No. 33, Moscow Oblast, RSFSR. ● Member, SupSov
Committee on Soviets of People's Deputies, Development of Govern-
ment, and Self-Government.

Stepanov, Vladimir Nikolaevich
● Director, "Vidlitsky" Livestock Sovkhoz, Olonetsky Raion. CPSU

member. Elected from TO No. 369, Karelian SSR. ● Made conservative speech at CPD; accused the forerunner of the MDG, the "Moscow group" of people's deputies (including historian Yurii Afanasev and economist Gavriil Popov), of leading Russia down the path of cooperatives, leasing and other "mistaken" ideas "without consulting the people" (*Pravda*, May 29, 1989).

Stoumova, Galina Ivanovna (F)
● Workshop chief, "Gatchinsky" Sovkhoz, Bolshie Kolpany, Gatchina Raion. CPSU member. Elected from TO No. 62, Leningrad Oblast, RSFSR. ● Member, CPD Drafting Commission; Council of the Union Planning and Budgetary Finance Commission.

Svatkovsky, Vladimir Vasilevich
● Chairman, V. I. Lenin Fishing Kolkhoz, Petropavlovsk-Kamchatsky, Kamchatka Oblast, RSFSR. CPSU member. Elected from the All-Union Association of Fishing Kolkhozes. ● Member, Council of the Union Planning and Budgetary Finance Commission.

Tetenov, Valentin Afanasevich
● First deputy chief, Perm Branch, Sverdlovsk Railroad. CPSU member. Elected from TO No. 256, Perm Oblast, RSFSR. ● Was 42 in June 1989; railway engineer. Nomination for chairman of the Council of the Union Commission on Transport was unsuccessfully opposed by deputies who said he knew nothing about information science (TASS, June 10, 1989). ● Member, USSR SupSov Presidium; chairman, Council of the Union Commission on Transport, Communications, and Information Science.

Timchenko, Mikhail Andreevich
● Director, "Marushinsky" Sovkhoz, Druzhba Settlement, Tselinnyi Raion. CPSU member. Elected from TO No. 67, Altai Krai, RSFSR. ● Election platform focused on local issues such as housing and road construction (*Sovetskaya Rossiya*, March 3, 1989). ● Member, SupSov Committee on Ecology and the Rational Use of Natural Resources.

Timchenko, Vladimir Mikhailovich
● Milling machine operator, "Azov Optiko-Mekhanichesky Zavod" Production Association, Azov. Elected from TO No. 271, Rostov Oblast, RSFSR. ● Member, Council of the Union Commission on Industry, Energy, and Technology.

Tsyplyaev, Sergei Alekseevich
● Scientific secretary, S. I. Vavilov State Optical Institute, Leningrad. CPSU member. Elected from the All-Union Komsomol. ● Member, SupSov Committee on Defense and State Security.

Tsyurupa, Viktor Aleksandrovich
● Head, Department of Ophthalmology, City Hospital No. 15, Moscow. Elected from TO No. 4, Moscow. ● Electoral platform focused on social issues and called for increased economic authority for local soviets (*Sovetskaya Rossiya*, April 21, 1989). In pre-CPD statement, argued that all CPD deputies should be allowed to participate in SupSov commissions and committees—at least in consultative role (*Vechernyaya Moskva*, May 17, 1989). ● Member, SupSov Committee on Public Health.

Tutov, Nikolai Dmitrievich
● Senior lieutenant; secretary, Komsomol committee, air force military unit, Orenburg. CPSU member. Elected from TO No. 244, Orenburg Oblast, RSFSR. ● Born 1961; Russian; graduated, Kiev Higher Military Engineering School. Member, armed forces since 1979. ● Member, SupSov Committee on Defense and State Security.

Usilina, Nina Andreevna (F)
● Chief veterinarian, "Komsomolets" Sovkhoz, Luzhaiki Settlement, Shakhunsky Raion. CPSU member. Elected from TO No. 165, Gorki Oblast, RSFSR. ● Member, SupSov Committee on Ecology and the Rational Use of Natural Resources.

Velikhov, Evgenii Pavlovich
● Vice president, USSR Academy of Sciences, Moscow. CPSU member. Elected from the CPSU. ● Born 1935; Doctor of Physical Mathematics. Member, CPSU CC since 1989. Director, Kurchatov Institute of Atomic Energy. Gorbachev's chief science adviser; has accompanied general secretary on numerous trips abroad. Identified by Western intelligence as coordinator of USSR's space defense program. Leader of campaign for computer education in USSR. Chairman, International Foundation for the Survival and Development of Humanity—the first nongovernmental organization to be granted independent status in the USSR. (Other founding members include Robert McNamara, Andrei

Sakharov, Roald Sagdeev, and Armand Hammer.) ● Member, CPD Constitutional Commission; SupSov Committee on Defense and State Security.

Veprev, Arkadii Filimonovich
● Director, "Nazarovsky" Sovkhoz, Nazarovsky Raion. CPSU member. Elected from TO No. 90, Krasnoyarsk Krai, RSFSR. ● Born 1927; higher education. Praised by Gorbachev in autumn of 1988 as outspoken and confident collective farm manager who had begun to lease land to the peasants on the family contract system. Honored in November 1988 with a state prize for his struggle against bureaucratic interference; Hero of Socialist Labor. For his impressions of the CPD, see *Sovetskaya Rossiya*, June 30, 1989. ● Member, USSR SupSov Presidium; chairman, SupSov Committee on Agrarian Questions and Food.

Vlazneva, Mariya Ivanovna (F)
● Milkmaid at the "Rossiya" Kolkhoz, Slaim, Torbeevsky Raion. Elected from TO No. 377, Mordovian ASSR.

Vnebrachnyi, Ivan Semenovich
● Diesel engine driver, Oktyabrsky Railroad's Velikie Luki Locomotive Depot, Velikie Luki, Pskov Oblast. CPSU member. Elected from TO No. 265, Pskov Oblast, RSFSR. ● Member, Council of the Union Commission on Transport, Communications, and Information Science.

Volkov, Vladimir Anatolevich
● Secretary, Party committee, M. I. Kalinin Machine Building Plant, Sverdlovsk. CPSU member. Elected from TO No. 294, Sverdlovsk Oblast, RSFSR. ● Spoke at the Nineteenth Party Conference in support of Eltsin; Sverdlovsk delegation disowned Volkov's statement, saying he had spoken without its authorization. Has advocated intensified conversion of defense production to civilian sector; *Sovetskaya Rossiya*, June 14, 1989. ● Member, Council of the Union Commission on Labor, Prices, and Social Policy.

Volodichev, Viktor Vasilevich
● Leader, team of construction workers on the "Angarstroi" Construction Work Train No. 274, Vikhorevka, Bratsky Raion, Irkutsk Oblast. CPSU member. Elected from TO No. 173, Irkutsk Oblast, RSFSR. ● Member, SupSov Committee on Construction and Architecture.

Voskoboinikov, Valerii Ivanovich
● Helicopter flight engineer, 25th Flight Detachment, Novyi Urengoi Combined Air Detachment. Elected from TO No. 324, Tyumen Oblast, RSFSR. ● At CPD in June 1989, proposed Boris Eltsin as alternative candidate to Gennadii Kolbin for post of chairman, USSR People's Control Commission. ● Member, Council of the Union Commission on Transport, Communications, and Information Science.

Yakutis, Vladislav Stanislavovich
● Leader of a large multiskilled team, "Boguchanles" Timber Association, Pinchuga Settlement, Boguchansky Raion. CPSU member. Elected from TO No. 93, Krasnoyarsk Krai, RSFSR. ● Member, SupSov Committee on Ecology and the Rational Use of Natural Resources.

Yarin, Veniamin Aleksandrovich
● Operator, V. I. Lenin Metallurgical Combine, Nizhnii Tagil. CPSU member. Elected from TO No. 302, Sverdlovsk Oblast, RSFSR.
● Outspoken worker whose recent statements propound a populist, Russian nationalist program for economic reform. In post-CPD roundtable discussion, declared economic reform would remain only words until local soviets were given legal rights to oversee economic activity; blasted ministries for keeping too tight a grip on the economy; did not, however, support Baltic proposals for territorial cost accounting on the grounds that the RSFSR was already lagging behind the Baltic states and would only fall further behind. Said workers in Western Siberia "can only dream of achieving what you in the Baltics already have" (*Baltimore Sun*, July 27, 1989). Critical of those who blame the CP for USSR's misfortunes (*Sovetskaya Rossiya*, June 14, 1989). During July 1989 miners' strikes, said that if he were in the Kuzbass or Donbass, he'd be with the strikers (Central Television, July 20, 1989).

Yarovaya, Olga Pavlovna (F)
● Milkmaid, "Krasnaya zvezda" Training Farm, Atkarsky Raion. CPSU member. Elected from TO No. 285, Saratov Oblast, RSFSR. ● Member, SupSov Committee on Women's Affairs, Family Protection, Motherhood, and Childhood.

Yudin, Vladimir Dmitrievich
● Chief, Central Geochemical Group, Northeastern Geological Produc-

tion Association Group, Khasyn Raion. CPSU member. Elected from TO No. 223, Magadan Oblast, RSFSR. ● Member, Council of the Union Commission on Development of Industry, Energy, Equipment, and Technology.

Zhdakaev, Ivan Andreevich
● Bulldozer operator, Pervomaisk Timber Industry Enterprise, Smirnykhovsky Raion. CPSU member. Elected from TO No. 291, Sakhalin Oblast, RSFSR. ● Member, Council of the Union Commission on Transport, Communications, and Information Science.

Zubov, Yurii Ivanovich
● Director, "Oktyabrsky" Sovkhoz, Rybinsky Raion. CPSU member. Elected from TO No. 348, Yaroslavl Oblast, RSFSR. ● Member, Council of the Union Planning and Budgetary Finance Commission.

Armenian SSR

Arutyunyan, Suren Gurgenovich
● First secretary, CC, CP of Armenia, Erevan. CPSU member. Elected from TO No. 737, Armenian SSR. ● Born September 5, 1939; Armenian; higher education; has worked in Party and government *apparat.* Appointed in 1988 as Party first secretary in Armenia after outbreak of ethnic conflict over Nagorno-Karabakh. Spoke at CPD in favor of establishment of joint-enterprise zone in his republic with foreign investment to rebuild areas destroyed by December 1988 earthquake (Central Television, May 31, 1989). ● Member, CPD Constitutional Commission.

Kirakosyan, Armenak Balasanovich
● Lathe operator at "Luis" Production Association's Lighting Engineering Plant, Kirovakan, Armenian SSR. Candidate CPSU member. Elected from the All-Union Komsomol. ● Member, SupSov Committee on Youth.

Voskanyan, Grant Mushegovich
● Chairman, Presidium, Armenian SSR SupSov, Erevan. CPSU member. Elected from TO No. 738, Armenian SSR. ● Born 1924; Armenian; trained as teacher before switching to Party work in 1959. Elected chairman, Presidium, Armenian SSR SupSov in December 1985. Argued in favor of

the transfer of Nagorno-Karabakh from Azerbaijan and in July 1988 expressed disappointment with SupSov refusal to transfer sovereignty to Armenia (TASS, July 18, 1988). ● Member, CPD Drafting Commission; deputy chairman, USSR SupSov Presidium.

Azerbaijan SSR

Amanov, Akif Mami ogly
● Drilling foreman, Drilling Work Administration, Ali-Bairamli. CPSU member. Elected from TO No. 675, Azerbaijan SSR. ● Member, Presidium, Azerbaijan SSR SupSov. Much-decorated "worker-hero"; delegate to two most recent CPSU Congresses (1981 and 1985). ● Member, Council of the Union Commission on Labor, Prices, and Social Policy.

Gilalzade, Dzhangir Gadi ogly
● Team leader, No. 32 Construction Administration, No. 3 Construction and Installation Trust, Kirovabad. CPSU member. Elected from TO No. 677, Azerbaijan SSR. ● Member, SupSov Committee on Construction and Architecture.

Melikov, Arif Dzhangir ogly
● Composer; department head, Azerbaijan State Conservatory, Baku. CPSU member. Elected from TO No. 681, Azerbaijan SSR.

Rzaev, Anar Rasul ogly
● Writer, first secretary, Azerbaijan Writers' Union Board, Baku. CPSU member. Elected from TO No. 671, Azerbaijan SSR. ● Born January 14, 1938; Azerbaijani; higher education in literature. Novelist and screenwriter; son of well-known Azerbaijani poets. Political moderate who avoided making a public statement during the Nagorno-Karabakh conflict. ● Member, SupSov Committee on Science, Public Education, Culture, and Upbringing.

Salimov, Alibala Khanakhmed ogly
● Chairman, N. Narimanov Kolkhoz, Neftechalinsky Raion, Azerbaijan SSR. CPSU member. Elected from the Council of Kolkhozes. ● Member, SupSov Committee on Agrarian Questions and Food.

Belorussian SSR

Bobritsky, Nikolai Grigorevich
● Deputy general director, "Bobruiskshina" Production Association, Bobruisk. CPSU member. Elected from TO No. 573, Mogilev Oblast, Belorussian SSR. ● Member, SupSov Committee on Economic Reform.

Dudko, Tamara Nikolaevna (F)
● Chairman, Partizansky Raiispolkom, Minsk, Belorussian SSR. CPSU member. Elected from the Soviet Women's Committee. ● Born 1945; Belorussian; higher education; engineer. For profile stressing women's concerns, see *Sovetskaya Belorussiya*, February 14, 1989. ● Member, CPD Drafting Commission; SupSov Committee on Soviets of People's Deputies, Development of Government, and Self-Government.

Feskov, Nikolai Stepanovich
● Director, Kochishche Secondary School, Elsky Raion. CPSU member. Elected from TO No. 558, Gomel Oblast, Belorussian SSR. ● Member, Council of the Union Planning and Budgetary Finance Commission.

Kalashnikov, Sergei Fedorovich
● Deputy director in charge of youth work at the F. E. Dzerzhinsky Bobruisk Sewn Goods Factory, Mogilev Oblast, Belorussian SSR. CPSU member. Elected from the All-Union Komsomol. ● Electoral statement defended informal youth groups that were "unfairly painted in black colors in the Belorussian press." Also said the Komsomol should not have a monopoly on youth activity (*Chyrvonaya zmena*, February 14, 1989). ● Member, SupSov Committee on Youth.

Luchenok, Igor Mikhailovich
● Composer; chairman, Belorussian SSR Composers' Union; Minsk. CPSU member. Elected from the USSR Trade Unions. ● Born 1938. Graduated Belorussian State Conservatory (1961). ● Member, SupSov Committee on International Affairs.

Miloserdnyi, Anatolii Kirillovich
● Director, "Krasnyi borets" Machine Tool Building Plant, Orsha. CPSU member. Elected from TO No. 553, Vitebsk Oblast, Belorussian SSR.
● Member, Council of the Union Commission on Planning, Budget, and Finance.

Piskunovich, Georgii Petrovich
- Machine operator, "Geroi Truda" Kolkhoz, Gluboksky Raion. Elected from TO No. 552, Vitebsk Oblast, Belorussian SSR. ● Member, Council of the Union Commission on Labor, Prices, and Social Policy.

Semukha, Vladimir Iosifovich
- Chairman, Belorussian SSR Red Cross Society CC, Minsk. CPSU member. Elected from the USSR Union of Red Cross and Red Crescent Societies. ● Member, SupSov Committee on Public Health.

Shetko, Pavel Vadimovich
- Lecturer, Propaganda Department, Minsk Obkom, Belorussian Komsomol. Elected from the All-Union Komsomol. ● Electoral platform focused on veterans' issues. Spoke at CPD on the "moral agony" of Afghan veterans (*Trud,* June 7, 1989). ● Member, SupSov Committee on Veterans and Invalids.

Sokolov, Efrem Evseevich
- First secretary, CC, CP of Belorussia, Minsk. CPSU member. Elected from TO No. 549, Brest Oblast, Belorussian SSR. ● Born April 25, 1926; Belorussian; graduated from Belorussian Agricultural Academy and Higher Party School. Specialist in agriculture who has spent the bulk of his career in the Belorussian CP organs. 1977–1987, first secretary, Brest Obkom. Highly praised (*Pravda,* October 30, 1986) prior to election to current post over heads of other local Party leaders. Member, CPSU CC since 1986. Originally viewed as leader in the "Gorbachev mold" and a strong supporter of *glasnost,* but has recently exhibited a conservative side: on the eve of the founding congress of the Belorussian Popular Front in June 1989, Sokolov attacked the Front's organizers as "extremist" and called on Party branches to deal severely with CP members who supported it (forcing the Front to hold its congress in Vilnius instead). *Pravda* (July 1, 1989) criticized the Belorussian Party and government for aloofness, intolerance and lack of democracy, mentioning Sokolov by name. Member of USSR SupSov (1984). ● Member, CPD Drafting Commission; CPD Constitutional Commission.

Estonian SSR

Lauristin, Marju (Lauristin, Maryu) (F)
● Head, Journalism Department, Tartu State University. CPSU member.
Elected from TO No. 750, Estonian SSR. ● Born 1940; Estonian; graduated from Tartu State University in philology. Daughter of first prime
minister of Communist Estonia (1940–1941). Together with fellow
deputy Ülo Vooglaid, Lauristin was active in the "New Left" movement
in the 1960s in Estonia. Founding member and leading theoretician of
PF of Estonia; the only SupSov deputy on its seven-person executive
committee, she has been a consistent proponent of Estonian sovereignty
and economic independence. Has called for official recognition that
Estonia was forcibly incorporated into the USSR in 1940. For a statement
of her positions, see her article in *The Independent*, July 31, 1989.
● Member CPD Drafting Commission, CPD Commission on the Molotov-
Ribbentrop Pact; Council of the Union Commission on Labor, Prices,
and Social Policy. Member, MDG.

Vare, Vello
● Major general; chief scientific associate, Institute of History, Estonian
SSR Academy of Sciences, Tallinn. CPSU member. Elected from the All-
Union Organization of War and Labor Veterans. ● Was 47 in June 1989;
Estonian; professor of military history. Favors allowing Estonians to
complete their military service in Estonia or neighboring Baltic states.
● Member, SupSov Committee on Defense and State Security.

Georgian SSR

Amaglobeli, Nodari Sardionovich
● Rector, Tbilisi State University. CPSU member. Elected from TO
No. 657, Georgian SSR. ● Was 55 in September 1985; Georgian; physicist
with higher education. Corresponding member, Georgian SSR Academy
of Sciences. Has held current post since 1985. ● Member, SupSov
Committee on International Affairs.

Kontselidze, Marina Rizaevna (F)
● Citrus fruit grower, Khala Village Kolkhoz, Kobuletsky Raion. CPSU
member. Elected from TO No. 659, Georgian SSR. ● Member, CPD
Drafting Commission; SupSov Committee on Youth.

Kublashvili, Vakhtang Vladimirovich
• Assembly fitter, Dimitrov Aircraft Production Association, Tbilisi. CPSU member. Elected from TO No. 656, Georgian SSR. • Member, CPD Mandate Commission; Council of the Union Commission on Development of Industry, Energy, Equipment, and Technology.

Kvaratskhelia, Gucha Shalvovna (F)
• Senior scientific associate, Institute of Linguistics, Georgian SSR Academy of Sciences; professor, Tbilisi State Pedagogical Institute. CPSU member. Elected from the Soviet Women's Committee.
• Member, SupSov Committee on Science, Public Education, Culture, and Upbringing.

Mgaloblishvili, Nodar Mikhailovich
• Architect; chairman, Georgian Architects' Union Board, Tbilisi. CPSU member. Elected from the USSR Architects' Union. • Born 1927; Georgian; graduated from Moscow Architecture Institute (1952). Former administrator, Tbilisi Academy of Arts; deputy, Georgian SSR SupSov. Failed in bid to become deputy chairman, Council of the Union, USSR SupSov, after several deputies objected to his claim that there was no anti-Russian feeling in Georgia (in connection with the April 1989 events in Tbilisi). In same speech, advocated economic sovereignty for all republics, including the RSFSR; called Gorbachev and Sakharov the "most outstanding people on the planet" (Central Television, June 10, 1989). • Member, SupSov Committee on Construction and Architecture.

Kazakh SSR

Dzhanasbaev, Azhibzhan Tokenovich
• Leader of a team of drillers, "Kazvolfram" Production Association's Akzhal Mine, Agadyrsky Raion. CPSU member. Elected from TO No. 627, Dzhezkazgan Oblast, Kazakh SSR. • Member, Council of the Union Commission on Labor, Prices, and Social Policy.

Chursina, Pavlina Mikhailovna (F)
• Weaver, Karagailinsky Cloth Combine, Fabrichnyi Settlement, Dzhambulsky Raion, Alma-Ata Oblast, Kazakh SSR. Elected from the Soviet Women's Committee. • Member, Council of the Union Planning and Budgetary Finance Commission.

Donchak, Yaroslav Antonovich
● Leader of a drift-mining team, "Sixtieth Anniversary of the October Revolution" Mine, Karaganda. CPSU member. Elected from TO No. 628, Karaganda Oblast, Kazakh SSR. ● Member, Council of the Union Commission on Labor, Prices, and Social Policy.

Fominykh, Viktor Nikolaevich
● Arc welder, "Aktyubinskselmash" Plant. Elected from TO No. 618, Aktyubinsk Oblast, Kazakh SSR. ● Pre-CPD statement expressed concern for ecology (*Pravda*, May 20, 1989). ● Member, Council of the Union Commission on Development of Industry, Energy, Equipment, and Technology.

Iskakova, Bayan Seilkhanovna (F)
● Chief of department, Kzyltu Raion Hospital, Kzyltu Workers' Settlement. CPSU member. Elected from TO No. 633, Kokchetav Oblast, Kazakh SSR. ● Was 32 in June 1989. ● Deputy chairman, Council of the Union, USSR SupSov.

Kolbin, Gennadii Vasilevich
● Chairman, USSR People's Control Committee. Elected from TO No. 624, Gurev Oblast, Kazakh SSR. ● Born May 7, 1927; Russian; qualified as engineer, Ural Polytechnic Institute (studied with Eltsin). Patronage of Andrei Kirilenko eased his way up hierarchy; held Party posts in Nizhnii Tagil, Sverdlovsk, and Ulyanovsk. 1975–1983, worked under Eduard Shevardnadze as second secretary of the CC of the Georgian CP; instituted a number of innovative economic and political experiments. Member, CPSU CC since 1981. Member of USSR SupSov (1984). Tough disciplinarian; model leader in Gorbachev mold. In December 1986, the appointment of the Russian Kolbin as successor to Dinmukhamed Kunaev to head the CP of Kazakhstan sparked two days of rioting by Kazakhs in Alma-Ata. In CPD elections in March 1989, however, Kolbin received 97 percent of the vote in his district. Appointed to head the watchdog People's Control Committee in June 1989. ● Member, CPD Constitutional Commission; member, USSR SupSov Presidium.

Krivoruchko, Ekaterina Vasilevna (F)
● Machine operator, Chimkent Cement Plant, Kazakh SSR. CPSU member. Elected from the Soviet Women's Committee. ● Member, SupSov Committee on *Glasnost*, Rights, and Appeals of Citizens.

Milkin, Anatolii Vasilevich
● First secretary, East Kazakhstan Obkom, Ust-Kamenogorsk. CPSU member. Elected from TO No. 621, Kazakh SSR. ● Born March 1930; Russian; graduated from Kazakh Mining and Metallurgy Institute (1952); Candidate of Technical Sciences. Has worked in Party and government posts in Kazakhstan since 1971; 1981–1984, chairman, Kazakh SSR People's Control Committee. Appointed to current post in December 1983. Member of USSR SupSov (1984). ● Member, Council of the Union Commission on Development of Industry, Energy, Equipment, and Technology.

Pal, Oskar Maksimovich
● Director, "Sovetskaya" Agrofirm, Vozvyshensky Raion. CPSU member. Elected from TO No. 640, North Kazakhstan Oblast, Kazakh SSR. ● Member, SupSov Committee on Economic Reform.

Sagdiev, Makhtai Ramazanovich
● Chairman, Presidium, Kazakh SSR SupSov. CPSU member. Elected from TO No. 632, Kokchetav Oblast, Kazakh SSR. ● Born 1929; Kazakh; graduated from Semipalatinsk Teaching Institute, Alma-Ata Higher Party School and Talgar Agricultural Technical School. Experience in Kazakh CP and government organs. 1985–1989, first secretary, Kokchetav Obkom. Member, CPSU CAC since 1986. Praised by then Kazakh Party leader Gennadii Kolbin for having won authority in his oblast (*Pravda*, April 24, 1988). ● Member, CPD Constitutional Commission; CPD Commission to Investigate the April 1989 Events in Tbilisi; deputy chairman, USSR SupSov Presidium.

Semenikhin, Aleksandr Vasilevich
● Electric locomotive mechanic, Tselinograd Station Locomotive Depot, Virgin Lands Railroad, Tselinograd. CPSU member. Elected from TO No. 647, Tselinograd Oblast, Kazakh SSR.

Shakhanov, Mukhtar
● Writer; secretary, Kazakh SSR Writers' Union Board; chief editor of the journal *Zhalyn*, Alma-Ata. CPSU member. Elected from TO No. 616, Alma-Ata Oblast, Kazakh SSR. ● Born 1942; Kazakh; graduate of Chimkent Pedagogical Institute. Pre-CPD statement called for creation of new governmental framework based on law (*Izvestia*, May 24, 1989). Raised the issue of December 1986 Alma-Ata riots in speech to CPD,

charging that the number of protesters killed was being concealed from the public; proposed setting up a commission to establish the truth (Central Television, June 6, 1989). ● Member, SupSov Committee on Ecology and the Rational Use of Natural Resources.

Shopanaev, Kaiyrly Amenovich

● Leader of a multiskilled team, Construction and Installation Administration No. 17, "Almaatakultbytstroi" Trust, Alma-Ata. CPSU member. Elected from TO No. 615, Alma-Ata. ● Expressed dismay that many CPSU deputies laid all the blame for Soviet economic crisis on the Party and Party apparatus (*Pravda*, June 19, 1989). ● Member, SupSov Committee on Construction and Architecture.

Suleimenov, Olzhas Omarovich

● Writer; first secretary, Kazakh Writers' Union Board. CPSU member. Elected from TO No. 642, Semipalatinsk Oblast, Kazakh SSR. ● Born 1936; Kazakh; graduate of Kazakh State University. Outstanding author and screenwriter. Independent-minded, outspoken activist on Kazakh ecological and social issues. Member of USSR SupSov (1984). At 1986 Soviet Writers' Congress asked why so little had been written about the millions of Soviet citizens who perished in the purges of the 1930s. Founder and chairman (1989) of "Nevada," an antinuclear organization aimed at closure of Semipalatinsk and analogous U.S. nuclear testing sites (TASS, March 22, 1989). Electoral platform said Kazakhstan should receive a higher proportion of revenue accruing from its natural resources (TASS, March 1, 1989). In CPD speech, called on Soviet authorities to recognize dissident thought as a creative, not hostile, factor (Central Television, June 8, 1989). ● Member, CPD Constitutional Commission; CPD Drafting Commission; CPD Commission to Investigate Materials Linked With the Activity of the USSR Prosecutor's Office Investigation Group Headed by Telman Gdlyan; SupSov Committee on Legislation, Legality, and Law and Order.

Kirgiz SSR

Druzhinina, Lyubov Nikolaevna (F)

● Sewing machine operator, May 1 Sewn Goods Production Association, Frunze, Kirgiz SSR. Elected from the USSR Trade Unions. ● Member, SupSov Committee on Women's Affairs, Family Protection, Motherhood, and Childhood.

Kerimbekov, Teldibek Abdievich
● Driver, Passenger Motor Transport Enterprise, Talas. CPSU
member. Elected from TO No. 722, Kirgiz SSR. ● Member, Council of
the Union Commission on Transport, Communications, and Information
Science.

Masaliev, Absamat Masalievich
● First secretary, CC, CP of Kirgizia, Frunze. CPSU member. Elected
from TO No. 716, Kirgiz SSR. ● Born 1933; Kirgiz; higher mining
and Party education. Member, CPSU CC since 1986. Extensive Party
and government experience; 1979–1985, first secretary, Issyk-Kul
Obkom; 1985–1986, inspector, CPSU CC. Appointed to current post
in November 1985; carried out purge of republican Buro and
Secretariat. Came under fire from central authorities in mid-1987 for
failure to call republican officials to account for economic stagnation.
At the Congress of People's Deputies, criticized those who "build their
political career on slandering prominent Party and government figures,"
giving negative image to Party personnel; complained "certain individuals" were launching an attack against the Party (Central Television,
May 31, 1989). Again defended role of Party in speech to CPSU CC
meeting (July 18, 1989), complaining about "irresponsibility
camouflaging itself as pluralism" (*Pravda*, July 21, 1989). ● Member,
CPD Constitutional Commission.

Latvian SSR

Gorbunovs, Anatolijs (Gorbunov, Anatolii Valeryanovich)
● Chairman, Presidium, Latvian SSR SupSov, Riga. CPSU member.
Elected from TO No. 713, Latvian SSR. ● Born 1942. Latvian; trained as
construction engineer. Active at an early age in Komsomol and worked
way up Party ranks to become Latvian CP CC ideology secretary in
1985. Described by Latvian intellectuals as a moderate reformer whose
positions have become increasingly progressive in recent years. On
behalf of Latvian deputies at CPD, presented draft law on Union-
republican sovereignty; in same speech, blamed overcentralization for
deteriorating ecological situation and living standards in his republic
(Central Television, May 31, 1989). ● Member, CPD Presidium; CPD
Drafting Commission; deputy chairman, USSR SupSov Presidium.

Skulme, Džemma (Skulme, Dzhemma Otovna) (F)
● Painter; chairman, Latvian SSR Artists' Association Board; secretary, USSR Artists' Union Board. CPSU member. Elected from the USSR Union of Artists. ● Born 1925; Latvian; graduated from Latvian State Academy of Arts. Member of USSR SupSov (1984). ● Member, Council of the Union Commission on Labor, Prices, and Social Policy.

Vagris, Jānis (Vagris, Yan Yanovich)
● First secretary, CC, CP of Latvia, Riga. CPSU member. Elected from TO No. 708, Latvian SSR. ● Born 1930; Latvian; higher education. Has worked for 30 years in Latvian Party and government. Was Latvian president until appointment to current position in October 1988. A moderate whose recent statements reflect an attempt to appeal both to Party authorities in Moscow and to public opinion at home. In an article commemorating the seventieth anniversary of the establishment of the Soviet republic of Latvia, asserted the Latvian people had made a "historic choice" in favor of socialism (*Pravda*, January 13, 1989). Promised to work for greater economic independence for Latvia in pre-election television interview (Central Television, March 24, 1989), but barely escaped defeat, winning only 51 percent of the vote. ● Member, CPD Constitutional Commission.

Lithuanian SSR

Antanaitis, Vaidotas (Vito)
● Forestry department head, Lithuanian Agricultural Academy, Noreikiskes Rural Soviet, Kaunas Raion. Elected from TO No. 689, Lithuanian SSR. ● Born July 27, 1928; Lithuanian; higher education. Active in the Lithuanian "Green" Movement. Member, Sajudis Sejm. ● Member, SupSov Committee on Ecology and the Rational Use of Natural Resources.

Brazauskas, Algirdas (Brazauskas, Algirdas-Mikolas Kaze)
● First secretary, CC, CP of Lithuania, Vilnius. CPSU member. Elected from TO No. 685, Lithuanian SSR. ● Born September 22, 1932; Lithuanian; higher education in economics. Extensive experience in republican Party and government. Not known for reformist views prior to Nineteenth CPSU conference, but has since presented himself as an advocate of reform and sought to win the favor of Sajudis. Called for a "sovereign

Lithuania" and Lithuanian as the official language at meeting in Vilnius (AP, June 25, 1988). In CPD speech on center-republic relations, complained the republics had been denied scope for independent action while the center had demonstrated its inability to manage the economy and solve ecological and social problems; called for recognition of the illegality of the secret protocol to the Molotov-Ribbentrop Pact (Central Television, May 31, 1989). ● Member, CPD Constitutional Commission; CPD Presidium.

Buračas, Antanas (Burachas, Antanas)
● Chairman, Scientific and Technical Information Council of the Presidium of the Lithuanian SSR Academy of Sciences, Vilnius. CPSU member. Elected from TO No. 687, Lithuanian SSR. ● Born June 17, 1939; Lithuanian. Doctor of Economics. Member, Sajudis inner council. ● Member, Council of the Union Planning and Budgetary Finance Commission.

Prunskienė, Kazimiera Danutė (Prunskene, Kazimira Danute Prano) (F)
● Deputy chairman, Lithuanian SSR Council of Ministers, Vilnius. CPSU member. Elected from TO No. 694, Lithuanian SSR. ● Born February 26, 1943; Lithuanian; graduated from Vilnius University; Doctor of Economics. Member, Sajudis inner council. Until appointment to current post in July 1989, was rector, Institute for Improving the Qualifications of National Economic Specialists of the Lithuanian SSR Council of Ministers. Vocal proponent of economic reform; one of the most knowledgeable and respected crusaders for republican economic independence. Radio Vilnius said her appointment as deputy chairman was designed to "ensure the economic independence of the republic and widen foreign economic links" (July 7, 1989). For her critique of draft law on republican self-financing, see *Sovetskaya Litva,* April 26, 1989. For CPD speech, see *Pravda,* June 9, 1989. ● Member, SupSov Committee on Economic Reform.

Moldavian SSR

Akhromeev, Sergei Fedorovich
● Adviser to the chairman, USSR SupSov (i.e., Mikhail Gorbachev). CPSU member. Elected from TO No. 697, Moldavian SSR. ● Born May 5, 1923; Russian; higher military education. Member, CPSU CC since 1983.

Member of USSR SupSov (1984). Chief of General Staff, USSR Armed Forces, and USSR first deputy minister of defense, 1984–1988. Hero of the Soviet Union. Key negotiator at sensitive US-Soviet arms talks; described by his U.S. negotiating partner Paul Nitze as "by far the most intellectually commanding figure on the Soviet military team." Initially opposed to Gorbachev's 18-month moratorium on nuclear arms testing; since 1987 has appeared fully supportive of Gorbachev's "new thinking." Testified, July 1989, before U.S. House of Representatives Armed Services Committee—the most senior Soviet official ever to stand before a U.S. congressional committee; see interview with *Washington Post*, July 24, 1989. Electoral platform stressed the need for continuing negotiations to reduce the level of military forces throughout the world (TASS, February 17, 1989). • Member, SupSov Committee on Defense and State Security.

Grossu, Semen Kuzmich

• First secretary, CC, CP of Moldavia, Kishinev. CPSU member. Elected from TO No. 699, Moldavian SSR. • Born March 18, 1934; Moldavian; higher education in agricultural economics. Member, CPSU CC since 1981. Longtime Party official; holdover from Brezhnev era. Has shown great hostility toward Moldavia's informal progressive movements, charging Moldavian university students with "political immaturity" for their allegedly nationalistic views. Repeatedly reprimanded in 1983–1986 by CPSU CC for poor economic management, padding of economic results, and "bureaucratic excesses." • Member, CPD Drafting Commission; CPD Constitutional Commission.

Katrinich, Vasilii Antonovich

• Team leader, "Fiftieth Anniversary of October" Kolkhoz, Kushmirka, Sholdanetsky Raion. CPSU member. Elected from TO No. 702, Moldavian SSR. • Moldavian; aged under 30. Former Afghan veteran turned pacifist who now says the Soviet Union should not invade foreign countries. Signed a letter with progressive Moldavian CPD deputies beseeching the Orthodox Patriarch in Moscow to replace the church representative in Moldavia (a Russian) with someone familiar with Moldavian language, culture, and history. Chastised local Party organization in the Moldavian city of Orgeev for dismissing a nationality-minded, reformist newspaper editor and petitioned CPSU CC to intervene in the matter (*Literatura și arta*, May 25 and June 29, 1989).

Mocanu, Alexandru (Mokanu, Aleksandr Aleksandrovich)
● CPSU member. Elected from TO No. 701, Moldavian SSR. ● Born 1934; Moldavian; graduated from Kishinev Agricultural Institute; Candidate of Economics. Was chairman, Moldavian SSR SupSov until election to current post in June 1989. Extensive experience in local government and Party organs in Moldavia since 1971. Member, CPSU CAC since 1986. Spoke at CPD on republican self-administration, nationality problems and ecological issues (*Pravda*, June 4, 1989). Moldavian activists see him as an adept politician who has adopted current populist positions.
● Deputy chairman, Council of the Union, USSR SupSov.

Tajik SSR

Kanoatov, Muminsho
● Writer; first secretary, Tajik SSR Writers' Union Board, Dushanbe. CPSU member. Elected from TO No. 724, Tajik SSR. ● Born 1932; Tajik; graduate, Tajik State University. Journalistic experience. Member of USSR SupSov (1984). ● Member, SupSov Committee on International Affairs.

Makhkamov, Kakhar
● First secretary, CC, CP of Tajikistan, Dushanbe. CPSU member. Elected from TO No. 723, Tajik SSR. ● Born 1932; Tajik; graduated Leningrad Mining Institute (1957). Extensive government experience; 1982–1985, chairman, Tajik SSR Council of Ministers; no full-time Party post until appointed to current position in December 1985. Member, CPSU CC since 1986. *Pravda* (December 31, 1987) criticized Tajik CP for "going through the motions of reform instead of tackling nepotism" and accused Makhkamov of uttering empty slogans. Speech at meeting of regional Party leaders (July 18, 1989) focused on ideological training of Party cadres and internal Party democracy (*Pravda*, July 21, 1989).
● Member, CPD Constitutional Commission.

Saidaliev, Saidkul
● Leader of a team of plasterers, No. 14 Special Construction Administration, "Dushanbestroi" Trust, Dushanbe. CPSU member. Elected from the USSR Trade Unions. ● Member, SupSov Committee on Construction and Architecture.

Turkmen SSR

Amanova, Maral Bazarovna (F)
● Department head, A. M. Gorki Turkmen State University, Ashkhabad. CPSU member. Elected from the Soviet Women's Committee. ● In pre-election program pledged to work for legislation enhancing women's social conditions and financial benefits (TASS, May 11, 1989). Has also expressed concern over ecology (*Pravda*, June 19, 1989). ● Member, Council of the Union Commission on Labor, Prices, and Social Policy.

Niyazov, Saparmurad Ataevich
● First secretary, CC, CP of Turkmenistan, Ashkhabad. CPSU member. Elected from TO No. 741, Turkmen SSR. ● Born 1940; Turkmen; graduated Leningrad Polytechnical Institute and Higher Party School. Member, CPSU CC since 1986. Appointed to current post in December 1985. Early career spent in Turkmen CC apparatus before appointed to head Ashkhabad Gorkom in 1980. Worked briefly in 1984 as an instructor in the Organizational Party Work Department of the CPSU CC. March 1985, chairman, Turkmen SSR Council of Ministers. In speech to CPD, praised Gorbachev and CPSU CC; declared that there was no desire for national exclusiveness in Turkmenistan but also commented on disproportion by which the republic supplies other Soviet republics with raw materials and receives an inferior amount of consumer products in return. Called for more economic responsibility for the Union-republics (*Izvestia*, June 3, 1989). ● Member, CPD Constitutional Commission.

Shaklycheva, Dzhumagozel (F)
● Leader of a team of plasterers and painters, "Maryoblagropromstroi" No. 22 Interfarm Mobile Mechanized Column, Dogryel Settlement, Sakar-Chaginsky Raion. Elected from TO No. 743, Turkmen SSR.

Ukrainian SSR

Amosov, Nikolai Mikhailovich
● Honorary director, Scientific Research Institute for Cardiovascular Surgery, Kiev. Elected from TO No. 64, Kiev. ● Was 76 in May 1989; heart specialist; corresponding member, USSR Academy of Medical Sciences. Holds progressive opinions on historical, ideological and

social issues. Advocates socialism with a human face (*Molod Ukrainy,* June 1, 1989). ● Member, SupSov Committee on Public Health.

Babchenko, Nikolai Ivanovich
● Chairman, Obkom of the Trade Union of Workers in Local Industry and Communal Service Enterprises, Dnepropetrovsk, Ukrainian SSR. CPSU member. Elected from the USSR Trade Unions. ● Member, SupSov Committee on Legislation, Legality, and Law and Order.

Breurosh, Boris Sergeevich
● Combine operator, "Druzhba" Kolkhoz, Palievka, Maloviskovsky Raion, Kirovograd Oblast. CPSU member. Elected from TO No. 479, Kirovograd Oblast, Ukrainian SSR.

Chabanov, Alim Ivanovich
● General director, "Rotor" Scientific Production Association, Cherkassy. CPSU member. Elected from TO No. 535, Cherkassy Oblast, Ukrainian SSR. ● Maverick enterprise manager. Lost job in 1985 following an industrial conflict. Factory workers resisted his attempts to introduce new technology and teamed with local Party officials to have him removed. Chabanov was supported by some local Party members whose letters to the CPSU CC were, however, intercepted by the regional authorities (i.e., the KGB). It took the intervention of Gorbachev himself to get Chabanov reinstated (Radio Moscow, June 17, 1986). He was later promoted to an even better post. Feature article in *Pravda* (January 31, 1988) praised his work at the "Rotor" association; for additional profile, see *Moscow News,* No. 5, 1988. ● Member, Council of the Union Planning and Budgetary Finance Commission.

Chentsov, Nikolai Ivanovich
● Arc welder, "Komsomolskoe" Mine Administration, Kirovskoe. Elected from TO No. 445, Donetsk Oblast, Ukrainian SSR. ● Member, Council of the Union Commission on Development of Industry, Energy, Equipment, and Technology.

Chepurnaya, Margarita Aleksandrovna (F)
● Organizer, Extracurricular and Extramural Education Work, Popovsky Secondary School, Konotopsky Raion. CPSU member. Elected from TO No. 514, Sumy Oblast, Ukrainian SSR. ● Member, SupSov Committee on Science, Public Education, Culture, and Upbringing.

Chervonopisky, Sergei Vasilevich
● First secretary, Cherkassy Komsomol Gorkom, Ukrainian SSR. CPSU member. Elected from the All-Union Komsomol. ● Afghan veteran who lost his legs in the war. Caused uproar at CPD when defended Afghan intervention and denounced Sakharov's statements on the subject as "irresponsible, inhuman and malevolent." Went on to criticize the People's Fronts as expressions of "national selfishness." Received standing ovation from CPD with closing affirmation of "the three words for which we must all fight: state power, statehood [*derzhava*], Communism" (Central Television, June 2, 1989). ● Member, SupSov Committee on International Affairs.

Danilov, Valerii Nikolaevich
● Foreman, refrigerated freight car depot, Pridneprovsk Railroad, Sinelnikovo. CPSU member. Elected from TO No. 430, Dnepropetrovsk Oblast, Ukrainian SSR. ● Member, Council of the Union Commission on Transport, Communications, and Information.

Demchenko, Fedor Mikhailovich
● Team leader, Poltava Housing Construction Combine. Elected from TO No. 504, Poltava Oblast, Ukrainian SSR. ● Member, SupSov Committee on Construction and Architecture.

German, Natalya Fedorovna (F)
● Team leader, "Shabo" Sovkhoz-Plant, Belgorod-Dnestrovsky Raion. Candidate CPSU member. Elected from TO No. 500, Odessa Oblast, Ukrainian SSR.

Gil, Yaroslav Yakovlevich
● Chief physician, Kremenets Central Raion Hospital. CPSU member. Elected from TO No. 517, Ukrainian SSR. ● Member, SupSov Committee on Public Health.

Grib, Aleksandr Vasilevich
● Blast furnace attendant, "Zaporozhstal" Metallurgical Combine, Zaporozhe. CPSU member. Elected from TO No. 454, Zaporozhe Oblast, Ukrainian SSR. ● Member, Council of the Union Commission on Labor, Prices, and Social Policy.

Kasyanov, Anatolii Fedorovich
● Chairman, Karl Marx Kolkhoz, Mariupol, Novoazovsky Raion, Donetsk Oblast, Ukrainian SSR. CPSU member. Elected from the Council of Kolkhozes. ● Member, Council of the Union Planning and Budgetary Finance Commission.

Kharchenko, Grigorii Petrovich
● First secretary, Zaporozhe Obkom. CPSU member. Elected from TO No. 459, Zaporozhe Oblast, Ukrainian SSR. ● Born 1936; Ukrainian; graduate of Moscow Institute of Rail Transport Engineering. One of a number of Ukrainian leaders who were active in the republic's Komsomol organization in the 1960s. Left Komsomol work in 1968; rose in the Zaporozhe apparatus until 1987, when he went to Moscow and the Organizational Party Work Department of the CPSU CC. Named to current post in October 1988. With Grigorii Revenko, one of only two Ukrainian obkom leaders elected to SupSov. ● Member, SupSov Committee on Defense and State Security.

Kravets, Vladimir Alekseevich
● Ukrainian SSR foreign minister, Kiev. CPSU member. Elected from TO No. 523, Kharkov Oblast, Ukrainian SSR. ● Born 1930; Ukrainian; higher education in international relations and history. Worked in Ukrainian CP CC apparatus. 1979–1984, permanent representative of the Ukrainian SSR to the United Nations. USSR ambassador extraordinary and plenipotentiary. ● Member, CPD Commission on the Molotov-Ribbentrop Pact; deputy chairman, SupSov Committee on International Affairs.

Kucherenko, Viktor Grigorevich
● Chairman, Donetsk Oblispolkom. CPSU member. Elected from TO No. 433, Donetsk Oblast, Ukrainian SSR. ● Born 1931; Ukrainian; higher education in metallurgy. Held Party and local government posts in Zhdanov and Donetsk before election to current position. ● Member, USSR SupSov Presidium; chairman, Council of the Union Planning and Budgetary Finance Commission.

Lesyuk, Yaroslav Stepanovich
● Chairman, Gnezdychevsky Settlement Ispolkom, Zhidachovsky Raion, Lvov Oblast, Ukrainian SSR. CPSU member. Elected from USSR Consumer Cooperatives. ● Member, SupSov Committee on Economic Reform.

Matiiko, Lidiya Timofeevna (F)
● Team leader, No. 37 Construction and Installation Administration, Fastov. CPSU member. Elected from TO No. 475, Kiev Oblast, Ukrainian SSR. ● Member, SupSov Committee on Construction and Architecture.

Matveichuk, Sergei Ivanovich
● Metalworker-repairman, cannery, Vladimir-Volynsky. CPSU member. Elected from TO No. 411, Volyn Oblast, Ukrainian SSR. ● Member, Council of the Union Commission on Development of Industry, Energy, Equipment, and Technology.

Moskalenko, Galina Semenovna (F)
● Link leader, Lenin Kolkhoz, Pogrebishchensky Raion. CPSU member. Elected from TO No. 407, Vinnitsa Oblast, Ukrainian SSR.

Moskalik, Mariya Nikolaevna (F)
● Cook, Gorodenkovsky Raion Consumers' Union Canteen, Ivano-Frankovsk Oblast, Ukrainian SSR. CPSU member. Elected from USSR Consumer Cooperatives.

Motornyi, Dmitrii Konstantinovich
● Chairman, S. M. Kirov Kolkhoz, Belozersky Raion, Kherson Oblast, Ukrainian SSR. CPSU member. Elected from the Council of Kolkhozes.
● Born 1927; Ukrainian; agricultural engineer. Has held current position since 1963. Twice Hero of Socialist Labor. Member, CPSU CAC, 1981–1986; member, CPSU CC since 1986.

Nozdrya, Viktor Alekseevich
● Leader, team of metalworkers and installation workers, "S. Ordzhoni-kidze Morskoi Zavod" Production Association, Sevastopol. CPSU member. Elected from TO No. 484, Crimean Oblast, Ukrainian SSR.
● Member, SupSov Committee on Soviets of People's Deputies, Development of Government, and Self-Government.

Opolinsky, Vladimir Aleksandrovich
● Team leader, Chernomorsky Ship Building Plant, Nikolaev, Ukrainian SSR. CPSU member. Elected from the USSR Trade Unions. ● Member, SupSov Committee on Defense and State Security.

Pavlevich, Ivan Borisovich
● Leader, "Desantnik" Military, Sports, and Patriotic Club, trade union committee of a housing association, Kamenets-Podolsky. CPSU member. Elected from TO No. 533, Khmelnitsky Oblast, Ukrainian SSR. ● Member, SupSov Committee on Youth.

Pavlyi, Aleksandr Andreevich
● Senior consultant, Donetsk Oblispolkom, Ukrainian SSR. CPSU member. Elected from the All-Union Organization of War and Labor Veterans. ● Member, Council of the Union Commission on Labor, Prices, and Social Policy.

Plyutinsky, Vladimir Antonovich
● Chairman, "Zarya Kommunizma" Kolkhoz, "Zarya" Agrofirm, Rovno Raion, Rovno Oblast, Ukrainian SSR. CPSU member. Elected from the Council of Kolkhozes. ● Born 1927; Polish; graduated from Lvov Agricultural Institute. Intelligence officer for partisan forces during World War II. Has worked in current position since 1963. Hero of Socialist Labor. Member of Ukrainian SSR SupSov (1985).

Prikhodko, Zinaida Semenovna (F)
● First secretary, Perechinsky Raikom, Transcarpathian Oblast, Ukrainian SSR. CPSU member. Elected from the Soviet Women's Committee. ● Member, SupSov Committee on Women's Affairs, Family Protection, Motherhood, and Childhood.

Revenko, Grigorii Ivanovich
● First secretary, Kiev Obkom. Elected from TO No. 470, Kiev Oblast, Ukrainian SSR. ● Born April 29, 1936; Ukrainian; graduated from Lvov Polytechnical Institute and Academy of Social Sciences of CPSU CC. Extensive experience in Ukrainian Komsomol and CP organs. Member, CPSU CC since 1986. One of the Ukrainian leaders who emerged from the republic's Komsomol organization. Career ties to Aleksandr Kapto (head of the CPSU CC Ideology Department): the two followed the same path through the Komsomol, Kiev Obkom, Ukrainian CP CC, and CPSU CC *apparats*. Revenko has strongly resisted calls to shut down the Chernobyl nuclear power plant, arguing that nuclear energy is vital to the economy of the republic; this is a controversial stance given the strong antinuclear ecological movement in the Ukraine. With Grigorii Kharchenko, one of only two Ukrainian obkom leaders elected to SupSov.

Ryabchenko, Sergei Mikhailovich
● Laboratory chief, Institute of Physics, Ukrainian SSR Academy of Sciences, Kiev. Elected from TO No. 468, Kiev. ● Doctor of Physical Mathematics. ● Member, SupSov Committee on Science, Public Education, Culture, and Upbringing. Member, MDG.

Saunin, Anatolii Nikolaevich
● Faculty lecturer, Makeevka Engineering Construction Institute, Donetsk. CPSU member. Elected from TO No. 443, Donetsk Oblast, Ukrainian SSR. ● Represents coal mining area where strikes broke out in July 1989. Spoke in support of radical "Moscow Group" of deputies to the CPD. Proposed parliamentary mechanism for expression of lack of confidence in the government (*Molod Ukrainy*, June 21, 1989). ● Member, MDG.

Sbitnev, Anatolii Mitrofanovich
● Steel worker, Kommunarsky Metallurgical Combine, Perevalsk. Elected from TO No. 414, Voroshilovgrad Oblast, Ukrainian SSR. ● Member, CPD Constitutional Commission, CPD Drafting Commission; Council of the Union Commission on Development of Industry, Energy, Equipment, and Technology.

Shabanov, Vitalii Mikhailovich
● Army general, USSR deputy minister of defense for armaments. CPSU member. Elected from TO No. 531, Khmelnitsky Oblast, Ukrainian SSR. ● Born January 1, 1923; Russian; graduated Leningrad Military Aviation Academy. Candidate of Technical Sciences. One of the USSR's leading armament experts, involved in development of modern military technology. Member, CPSU CC since 1983. In rare interview, said Soviet military spending was being reduced (*Washington Post*, July 27, 1988). Member of USSR SupSov (1984). Possible links to Gorbachev adviser Sergei Akhromeev. ● Member, SupSov Committee on Defense and State Security.

Sharyi, Grigorii Ivanovich
● Chairman, "Zapovit Lenina" Kolkhoz, Chutovsky Raion, Poltava Oblast, Ukrainian SSR. CPSU member. Elected from the All-Union Komsomol. ● Member, SupSov Committee on *Glasnost*, Rights, and Appeals of Citizens.

Shcherbak, Yurii Nikolaevich
● Writer; secretary, Ukrainian Writers' Union Board, Kiev. Elected from TO No. 469, Kiev. ● Was 55 in June 1989; Ukrainian; graduate of Kiev Medical Institute. Worked until 1987 at Kiev Scientific Research Institute of Epidemiology and Infectious Diseases. Prolific novelist and screenwriter who has received many awards for his literary work. Emerged at CPD as leader of attack against nuclear power. Pre-CPD interview revealed growing dissatisfaction with the political, economic, and, above all, ecological situation in Ukraine (*Robitnycha hazeta*, April 8, 1989). Chairman of the "Zeleniy svit" (Green World) ecological association—an organization that aims to prevent despoiling of the Ukrainian countryside by grandiose industrial and energy projects. Active in the Ukrainian PF. Political stance is that of a reforming populist supportive of evolutionary reform of the Soviet system. ● Member, CPD Secretariat; SupSov Committee on Ecology and the Rational Use of Natural Resources. Member, MDG.

Shust, Anna Andreevna (F)
● Livestock unit chief, "Mayak" Kolkhoz, Sumy Raion, Sumy Oblast, Ukrainian SSR. CPSU member. Elected from the Soviet Women's Committee.

Sidorchuk, Tatyana Vasilevna (F)
● Upholsterer, Carpathian Furniture Combine, Ivano-Frankovsk. Elected from TO No. 460, Ivano-Frankovsk Oblast, Ukrainian SSR. ● Member, MDG.

Smirnov, Dmitrii Genrikhovich
● Construction engineer, "KhEMZ" Production Association, Kharkov. CPSU member. Elected from TO No. 521, Kharkov Oblast, Ukrainian SSR. ● Was 30 in June 1989. Expressed concern at hatred directed against Sakharov at the CPD, saying that, although he did not agree with Sakharov in all respects, he felt sympathy for the "great scholar" (*Molod Ukrainy*, June 22, 1989). ● Member, Council of the Union Planning and Budgetary Finance Commission. Member, MDG.

Sukhov, Leonid Ivanovich
● Taxi-driver, Kharkov 16301 Motor Transport Enterprise, Solonitsevka Settlement, Dergachevsky Raion. Elected from TO No. 519, Kharkov Oblast, Ukrainian SSR. ● Electoral platform complained of ecological

damage caused by traffic in cities (*Izvestia*, March 29, 1989). Stunned CPD by comparing Gorbachev to Napoleon and warning of the harmful influence wielded on Gorbachev by "sycophants" and his wife (Central Television, May 26, 1989). Proposed Eltsin for chairman of People's Control Committee (Central Television, June 7, 1989). ● Member, Council of the Union Commission on Transport, Communications, and Information Science. Member, MDG.

Sushko, Boris Ivanovich
● Smelter, "Fiftieth Anniversary of the USSR" Pure Metals Plant, Svetlovodsk, Kirovograd Oblast, Ukrainian SSR. CPSU member. Elected from the All-Union Society of Inventors and Rationalizers. ● Member, Council of the Union Commission on Development of Industry, Energy, Equipment, and Technology. Member, MDG.

Trefilov, Viktor Ivanovich
● Vice president, Ukrainian SSR Academy of Sciences; director, Institute of Problems of Materials Science, Ukrainian SSR Academy of Sciences, Kiev. CPSU member. Elected from the USSR Union of Scientific and Engineering Societies. ● Born 1930; Russian; graduated Kiev Polytechnical Institute. Doctor of Physical Mathematics. Has worked in Ukrainian SSR Academy of Sciences since 1953; vice president since 1974. Member of Ukrainian SupSov (1985). ● Member, CPD Drafting Commission; SupSov Committee on Science, Public Education, Culture, and Upbringing.

Tsarevsky, Aleksandr Leonidovich
● Face worker, "Twenty-second CPSU Congress" Mine of the "Stakhanovugol" Production Association, Stakhanov, Voroshilovgrad Oblast, Ukrainian SSR. CPSU member. Elected from the All-Union Komsomol. ● Member, SupSov Committee on Youth.

Tsavro, Yurii Stanislavovich
● Head of department, Yalta City Hospital. CPSU member. Elected from TO No. 485, Crimea Oblast, Ukrainian SSR. ● Member, MDG.

Tsybukh, Valerii Ivanovich
● CPSU member. Elected from TO No. 408, Vinnitsa Oblast, Ukrainian SSR. ● Born March 9, 1951; Ukrainian; graduate of Kiev Engineering Construction Institute and Higher Party School. Held several posts in Ukrainian Komsomol before being named first secretary in 1986;

resigned from this post in view of new job as chairman of SupSov youth committee. Denied that his committee will be a Komsomol lobby in the SupSov, saying the Komsomol has no inherent right to leadership of the country's youth (TASS, June 19, 1989). ● Member, USSR SupSov Presidium; chairman, SupSov Committee on Youth.

Tyminsky, Grigorii Aleksandrovich
● Chairman, "Druzhba narodov" Kolkhoz, Kelmenetsky Raion. CPSU member. Elected from TO No. 545, Chernovtsy Oblast, Ukrainian SSR.
● Member, SupSov Committee on Construction and Architecture.

Vakarchuk, Ivan Aleksandrovich
● Department head, Lvov State University. CPSU member. Elected from TO No. 486, Lvov Oblast, Ukrainian SSR. ● Member, SupSov Committee on Science, Public Education, Culture, and Upbringing.

Vasilchuk, Nikolai Parfenovich
● Chairman, Khmelnitsky Oblast Consumer Cooperative Union Board, Ukrainian SSR. CPSU member. Elected from the USSR Consumer Cooperatives.

Vasilets, Aleksandr Nikolaevich
● Engine driver, "Twenty-fifth CPSU Congress" Southern Railroad Locomotive Depot, Kupyansk. CPSU member. Elected from TO No. 526, Kharkov Oblast, Ukrainian SSR. ● Member, Council of the Union Commission on Transport, Communications, and Information Science.

Vologzhin, Valentin Mikhailovich
● General director, "Konveier" Production Association, Lvov, Ukrainian SSR. Elected from the USSR Union of Scientific and Engineering Societies. ● Was 52 in July 1989; metallurgical engineer. In 1988, the association he heads became the USSR's first joint stock enterprise since the 1920s. ● Member, USSR SupSov Presidium; chairman, SupSov Committee on Economic Reform.

Vuichitsky, Anatolii Stanislavovich
● Chairman, "Druzhba" Kolkhoz, Novomoskovsky Raion, Dnepropetrovsk Oblast. CPSU member. Elected from TO No. 429, Dnepropetrovsk Oblast, Ukrainian SSR. ● Member, SupSov Committee on Agrarian Questions and Food.

Yakimenko, Anatolii Nikolaevich
● Chairman, "Zhovten" Kolkhoz, Novgorod-Seversky Raion.CPSU member. Elected from TO No. 543, Chernigov Oblast, Ukrainian SSR.

Zelinsky, Igor Petrovich
● Rector, Odessa State University. CPSU member. Elected from TO No. 497, Odessa Oblast, Ukrainian SSR. ● For short statement on establishing true economic independence for soviets, see *Sovetskaya Rossiya*, May 31, 1989. ● Member, SupSov Committee on Science, Public Education, Culture, and Upbringing.

Uzbek SSR

Akbarov, Yuldash Tadzhievich
● Driver, No. 2 Motor Vehicle Combine, Tashkent. CPSU member. Elected from TO No. 596, Tashkent Oblast, Uzbek SSR. ● Complained at CPD that Congress was wasting time due to the "demagoguery" of certain deputies (*Izvestia*, May 28, 1989). ● Member, Council of the Union Commission on Transport, Communications, and Information Science.

Arslonov, Alier Kumrievich
● Team leader, "Twenty-second CPSU Congress" Kolkhoz, Namangan Oblast, Uzbek SSR. CPSU member. Elected from TO No. 585, Namangan Oblast, Uzbek SSR. ● Member, Council of the Union Planning and Budgetary Finance Commission.

Ergashev, Bakhromzhon Makhmudovich
● Chairman, Engels Kolkhoz, Leningradsky Raion, Fergana Oblast, Uzbek SSR. CPSU member. Elected from the Council of Kolkhozes.

Kirgizbaeva, Tukhtakhon Bazarovna (F)
● Team leader, "Malik" Sovkhoz, Syr-Darinsky Raion, Syr-Darya Oblast, Uzbek SSR. CPSU member. Elected from the CPSU. ● Born 1942; Uzbek; higher agricultural education. Member, CPSU CC since 1989. ● Member, SupSov Committee on Veterans and Invalids.

Kuchersky, Nikolai Ivanovich

● Director, "Fiftieth Anniversary of the USSR" Mining and Metallurgical Combine, Navoi. CPSU member. Elected from TO No. 588, Samarkand Oblast, Uzbek SSR. ● Member, SupSov Committee on Defense and State Security.

Mirkasymov, Mirakhmat Mirkhadzhievich

● First secretary, Tashkent Obkom. CPSU member. Elected from TO No. 604, Tashkent Oblast, Uzbek SSR. ● Uzbek. Gained current post in September 1988 as a "new blood" appointment in Moscow's effort to assert control over the Central Asian republics. Lively, innovative leader who progressed within the space of one year from Party leader in Uzbekistan's tiny but heavily populated Khorezm Oblast to first secretary of the republic's major cultural and industrial region: the capital, Tashkent. Elected to CPD and to SupSov, no mean achievement for a regional Party leader. ● Member, Council of the Union Commission on Development of Industry, Energy, Equipment, and Technology.

Mukhtarov, Akhmedzhan Gulyamovich

● Editor, newspaper *Kishlok khakikati* (Rural Truth), Tashkent; chairman, Uzbek Journalists' Union Board. CPSU member. Elected from the USSR Journalists' Union. ● Was 53 in May 1989. Higher education in philology. Member, Uzbek CP CAC. ● Member, Council of the Union Planning and Budgetary Finance Commission.

Ogarok, Valentin Ivanovich

● First deputy chairman, Uzbek SSR Council of Ministers, Tashkent. CPSU member. Elected from TO No. 581, Kashka-Darya Oblast, Uzbek SSR. ● Member, Council of the Union Planning and Budgetary Finance Commission.

Pavlov, Aleksandr Sergeevich

● Chief, CPSU CC State and Legal Department, Moscow. CPSU member. Elected from TO No. 602, Tashkent Oblast, Uzbek SSR. ● Since early 1980s, worked in CPSU CC Administrative Organs Department, which supervised military, security, intelligence, and legal institutions. Pavlov was appointed to head department when it was reorganized and renamed in 1988. ● Member, CPD Constitutional Commission; CPD Constitutional Oversight Commission; SupSov Committee on Legislation.

Rakhimov, Azim
● Deputy manager, "Bukharaoblagropromstroi" No. 2 Oblast State Cooperative Association, Bukhara, Uzbek SSR. CPSU member. Elected from the All-Union Organization of War and Labor Veterans.

Salykov, Kakimbek
● CPSU member. Elected from TO No. 612, Karakalpak ASSR.
● Born 1932; Kazakh; graduated from Moscow's Precious Metals and Gold Institute and Higher Party School. Author of seven volumes of poetry. Member, CPSU CC since 1986. Early career spent in Kazakhstan; 1975–1984, CPSU CC inspector (responsible for Central Asia); 1984, sent to Karakalpak ASSR as Party first secretary; orchestrated purge of local government and Party apparatus as part of republican-wide campaign against corruption. Described by TASS as active environmentalist campaigning for preservation of Aral Sea (June 10, 1989). Gave up his Party post when appointed to chairmanship of SupSov committee in June 1989. ● Member, CPD Mandate Commission; member, USSR SupSov Presidium; chairman, SupSov Committee on Ecology and the Rational Use of Natural Resources.

Ubaidullaeva, Rano Akhatovna (F)
● Deputy director, Economics Institute, Uzbek SSR Academy of Sciences, Tashkent. CPSU member. Elected from the Soviet Women's Committee.
● Member, Council of the Union Commission on Labor, Prices, and Social Policy.

Yusupov, Erkin Yusupovich
● Vice president, Uzbek SSR Academy of Sciences, Tashkent. CPSU member. Elected from the All-Union "Znanie" Society. ● Born 1929; Uzbek; Doctor of Philosophy. During December 1986 Alma-Ata riots, denounced "Islamic nationalism" and called for improving the "atheistic and internationalistic education of the masses" (*Washington Times*, February 2, 1987). During June 1989 unrest in Fergana, condemned the role of "extremists" and informal organizations in kindling the strife and "distorting the nationalities policy of the Soviet Communist Party and the role of the Russian people in the fate of our country" (TASS, August 7, 1989). ● Member, CPD Drafting Commission; CPD Accounting Commission; SupSov Committee on International Affairs.

Zhurabaeva, Tozhikhon (F)
● Chief, Rural Outpatients' Clinic of the Naiman Kishlak Soviet, Tashlaksky Raion. Elected from TO No. 607, Fergana Oblast, Uzbek SSR.
● Member, SupSov Committee on Women's Affairs, Family Protection, Motherhood, and Childhood.

3

The Council of Nationalities

From the Russian Soviet Federated Socialist Republic (RSFSR)

Belov, Vasilii Ivanovich
● Writer; secretary, RSFSR Writers' Union, Vologda. CPSU member. Elected from the CPSU. ● Born October 23, 1932. One of the best-known and most influential of Russian nationalist writers. In early 1960s, a leading figure of the "village prose" literary movement, which focused on life in rural Russia. His works are especially sympathetic to the plight of the Russian peasantry during collectivization. Has recently come under fire from those who allege his works are anti-Semitic and chauvinistic. Public stance combines conservative political views with some reformist economic proposals. Supportive of Pamyat and other groups that rally for a revival of Russian nationalist culture. Coauthor of letter to *Pravda* (November 9, 1987) on the harmful effects of rock music and television on the morals of Soviet youth. Election platform called for freeing industry and agriculture from bureaucratic tutelage but warned against the import of Western economic solutions (*Pravda*, March 5, 1989). ● Member, SupSov Committee on Agrarian Questions and Food.

Bosenko, Nikolai Vasilevich
● Chairman, All-Russian Council of War and Labor Veterans, Moscow. CPSU member. Elected from All-Union Organization of War and Labor Veterans. ● Born 1918; war veteran. From 1961, held Party posts in Stavropol Krai (Gorbachev's home territory); chairman, Stavropol Kraiispolkom for five years; 1973–1985, chairman, RSFSR State Committee for Supply of Production Equipment for Agriculture; 1985, retired on pension. Complained that millions of Soviet veterans and disabled persons were living in miserable conditions and called on the government to correct this injustice (*Izvestia*, July 23, 1989). ● Member, CPD Mandate Commission; member, USSR SupSov Presidium; chairman, SupSov Committee on Veterans and Invalids.

Eltsin, Boris Nikolaevich
● CPSU member. Elected from NTO No. 1, Moscow. ● Born February 1, 1931; Russian; graduated as construction engineer from Ural Polytechnic Institute. Extensive industrial and Party experience in native Sverdlovsk. Member, CPSU CC since 1981. Brought into CC *apparat* in Moscow in 1985 to oversee construction; later that year appointed to head the Moscow City Party organization where he began to clean up the corruption rampant under his predecessor, Viktor Grishin. Outspoken reformer and opponent of official privilege; disciplinarian and populist. Unrelenting critic of Party conservatives, notably his one-time patron, Egor Ligachev. Appointed candidate member of CPSU Politburo in 1986, but dismissed in disgrace from the Politburo and from his Moscow post a year later and appointed first deputy chairman, State Construction Committee; relinquished this post in 1989 to run for election as Moscow's deputy to the CPD in 1989; he won with 89.6 percent of the vote. This unprecedented political comeback made Eltsin a force the Kremlin could not afford to ignore. ● Member, USSR SupSov Presidium; chairman, SupSov Committee on Construction and Architecture; member, CPD Constitutional Commission. In July 1989, elected one of five chairmen of the MDG "progressive faction" in the CPD; told reporters the group would promote radical change through work inside and outside the CPD.

Falin, Valentin Mikhailovich
● Chief, CPSU CC International Department, Moscow. CPSU member. Elected from the Union of Soviet Societies for Friendship and Cultural Relations with Foreign Countries and the Soviet Society for Cultural Ties with Compatriots Abroad (the "Rodina" Society). ● Born April 3, 1926; Russian; graduate of Moscow Institute for International Relations. Member, CPSU CC since 1989. Leading Soviet expert on Western Europe (FRG in particular). Has held numerous government and Party posts in the area of foreign relations. 1971–1978, USSR ambassador to the Federal Republic of Germany; 1978–1983, first deputy chief, International Information Department, CPSU CC; 1983–1986, political observer, *Izvestia*; 1986–1988, chairman, Novosti Press Agency (APN); since 1988, chief, CPSU CC International Department, and member, CPSU CC Commission on International Policy. As head of International Department, Falin succeeded Anatolii Dobrynin, whose lack of knowledge of machinery of CC *apparat* made him a weak department head. Falin seems to have been appointed because his past experience

enabled him to "work the system." As member of CPD Commission on Molotov-Ribbentrop Pact, Falin confirmed the existence of a secret protocol to the treaty (*Die Welt*, July 23, 1989), reversing his previous assertions that the document could not be found and therefore could not be said to have existed. • Member, CPD Commission on the Molotov-Ribbentrop Pact; SupSov Committee on International Affairs.

Gaer, Evdokiya Aleksandrovna (F)
• Junior scientific associate, Institute of History, Archeology and Ethnography, Far Eastern Branch, USSR Academy of Sciences, Vladivostok. CPSU member. Elected from NTO No. 8, RSFSR. • Was 55 in June 1989; Nanian; higher education. Bold, outspoken intellectual who defeated the commander of the Far Eastern military district for CPD seat. Defended Sakharov at CPD in the uproar over his comments on Afghanistan (Central Television, June 2, 1989). Lost bid for post of deputy chairman, SupSov Council of Nationalities. Much concerned with ecological issues and preservation of the identity of the small nations of the USSR. For profiles, see *Moskovskie novosti*, No. 26, 1989; *Pravda*, June 26, 1989. • Member, Council of Nationalities Commission on Nationality Policy and Interethnic Relations. Founding member, MDG.

Likhanov, Albert Anatolevich
• Writer; chairman, V. I. Lenin Soviet Children's Foundation Board, Moscow. CPSU member. Elected from the Soviet Children's Foundation. • Was 54 in August 1989. Former editor of magazine *Smena*. Prominent crusader on social issues. Revealed startling statistics on youth crime, drug abuse, and venereal disease at founding conference of Soviet Children's Foundation in October 1987 (*Semya*, January 1988). Spoke at CPD about high rates of infant mortality, child homelessness, and juvenile crime (Central Television, June 1, 1989). At SupSov, proposed revocation of Leonid Brezhnev's "Order of Victory" (TASS, June 26, 1989). • Member, CPD Constitutional Commission; SupSov Committee on Science, Public Education, Culture, and Upbringing.

Lukin, Vladimir Petrovich
• Oxyacetylene cutter, V. V. Kuibyshev Diesel Engine Building Plant, Kolomna. CPSU member. Elected from NTO No. 2, Moscow Oblast. • Member, CPD Commission to Investigate the April 1989 Events in Tbilisi; SupSov Committee on Defense and State Security.

Matyukhin, Leonid Ivanovich
● Chief, Gorki Railroad. CPSU member, Elected from NTO No. 6, Gorki.
● Member, SupSov Committee on Economic Reform.

Nevolin, Sergei Innokentevich
● Chief physician, Novokuznetsk City Hospital No. 11. CPSU member.
Elected from NTO No. 13, Kemerovo. ● Member, SupSov Committee on
Public Health.

Podziruk, Viktor Semenovich
● Lieutenant colonel, senior instructor, navigator-researcher in a military
unit, Ivanovo Oblast. CPSU member. Elected from NTO No. 9, Ivanovo.
● Born 1944; Russian; higher military education; journalism degree from
Tartu State University. Maverick army officer with no combat experience
whose election platform called for introduction of all-professional army
and abolition of student draft (*Washington Post*, March 24, 1989); in
CPD elections, defeated Boris Snetkov, the commander of Soviet forces
in Germany and decorated World War II veteran who was supported by
local Party officials and the military establishment. Podziruk was critical
of military practices during the SupSov confirmation hearings for
minister of defense Dmitrii Yazov (*Krasnaya zvezda*, July 4; July 11,
1989). ● Member, SupSov Committee on Defense and State Security.

Vorotnikov, Vitalii Ivanovich
● Chairman, Presidium, RSFSR SupSov, Moscow. CPSU member. Elected
from NTO No. 5, Voronezh. ● Born January 20, 1926; Russian; trained as
aviation engineer. Extensive background in Party work in industry in the
RSFSR. Member, CPSU CC since 1971. Member of USSR SupSov (1984).
Orthodox Party *apparatchik* who favors safe, middle-of-the-road
positions. Despite speeches and articles in support of *perestroika* and
democratization, seen by many as a member of the Politburo's conservative wing. Career took a downturn in 1979 when he was dispatched for
three years to Cuba as Soviet ambassador; returned to responsible Party
work following Andropov's rise to power. Member, Politburo, since
1983. Vorotnikov was the only Politburo member elected to the SupSov
(of which Gorbachev and Lukyanov are not technically members).
● Member, CPD Presidium; CPD Constitutional Commission; deputy
chairman, USSR SupSov Presidium.

From the Armenian SSR

Abramyan, Khoren Babkenovich
● Artistic leader, Sundukyan Academic Drama Theater; chairman, Armenian Theater Workers' Union Board, Erevan. Elected from the USSR Theater Workers' Union. ● Was 58 in May 1989; Armenian. Electoral platform spoke of importance of artistic expression in strengthening society (*Sovetskaya Rossiya*, May 1, 1989). ● Member, Council of Nationalities Commission on the Development of Culture, Language, National and Interethnic Traditions, and Preservation of Historical Heritage.

Ambartsumyan, Sergei Aleksandrovich
● Rector, Erevan State University. CPSU member. Elected from NTO No. 392, Armenian SSR. ● Born 1922; Armenian; Doctor of Technical Sciences. Member of USSR SupSov (1984). Member of a team of Armenian representatives who met with Gorbachev to discuss the NKAO conflict (*Washington Post*, October 20, 1988). ● Member, CPD Constitutional Commission; SupSov Committee on International Relations.

Ambartsumyan, Viktor Amazaspovich
● President, Armenian SSR Academy of Sciences, Erevan. CPSU member. Elected from NTO No. 404, Armenian SSR. ● Born 1908; Armenian. World-famous astrophysicist; graduate of Leningrad State University; Doctor of Physical Mathematics. Member of USSR SupSov (1984). One of the early leaders of the unofficial "Karabakh Committee" whose aim was to transfer control of Nagorno-Karabakh from Azerbaijan to Armenia. Soon dissociated himself, but stood his ground as Armenian representative when berated by Gorbachev in July 1988 at meeting of Presidium of USSR SupSov that was devoted to Nagorno-Karabakh question; reminded the "young man" (Gorbachev) that he was an 80-year-old scientist who had no interest in petty nationalism (*Pravda*, July 20, 1988). ● Member, SupSov Committee on Economic Reform; CPD Presidium.

Arutyunyan, Elmir Tatulovich
● Leader of a team of toolmakers, "Elektropribor" Production Association, Erevan. CPSU member. Elected from NTO No. 391, Armenian SSR. ● Armenian. ● Member, SupSov Committee on *Glasnost*, Rights and Appeals of Citizens.

Arutyunyan, Lyudmila Akopovna (F)
● Department head, Erevan State University. CPSU member. Elected from the Soviet Women's Committee. ● Armenian; teacher of philosophy with higher education. Called at CPD for new mechanism for mediating interethnic disputes (*Izvestia*, June 9, 1989). ● Member, CPD Commission on Molotov-Ribbentrop Pact; Council of Nationalities Commission on Nationality Policy and Interethnic Relations.

Enokyan, Goarik Agabekovna (F)
● General director, "Garun" Sewn Goods Production Association, Erevan. CPSU member. Elected from NTO No. 387, Armenian SSR. ● Member, Council of Nationalities Commission on Consumer Goods, Trade, and Communal and Household Services for the Population.

Igityan, Genrikh Surenovich
● General director, Republican Center of Aesthetic Education; director, Armenian Museum of Modern Art, Erevan. Elected from the USSR Artists' Union. ● Armenian. Progressive intellectual. ● Member, SupSov Committee on Science, Public Education, Culture, and Upbringing. Member, MDG.

Khanzadyan, Sero Nikolaevich
● Writer, Erevan. CPSU member. Elected from NTO No. 416, Armenian SSR. ● Member, SupSov Committee on Veterans and Invalids.

Mnatsakanyan, Bavakan Gagikovna (F)
● Chairman, Arshaluis Rural Soviet, Echmiadzin Raion, Armenian SSR. CPSU member. Elected from USSR Consumer Cooperatives. ● Born 1955; Armenian. Member of USSR SupSov (1984).

Oganesyan, Rafik Gevorkovich
● Bricklayer, "Lenstroi" Trust No. 46 Construction Administration, Leninakan. Elected from NTO No. 395, Armenian SSR. ● Armenian. ● Member, SupSov Committee on Construction and Architecture.

Vardanyan, Rafik Petrosovich
● Chairman, Shaumyan Kolkhoz, Ararat. CPSU member. Elected from NTO No. 400, Armenian SSR. ● Member, Council of Nationalities Commission on Social and Economic Development of Union and Autonomous Republics, and Autonomous Oblasts and Okrugs.

From the Azerbaijan SSR

Abbasov, Yashar Isag ogly
● Steelworker, V. I. Lenin Pipe Rolling Mill, Sumgait, Azerbaijan SSR.
CPSU member. Elected from the USSR Trade Unions. ● Azerbaijani.
● Member, SupSov Committee on Ecology and the Rational Use of
Natural Resources.

Aleskerova, Rukhi Mursal kyzy (F)
● Chairman, Lagich Settlement Ispolkom, Ismaillinsky Raion. CPSU
member. Elected from NTO No. 205, Azerbaijan SSR. ● Member, CPD
Drafting Commission; SupSov Committee on Soviets of People's Deputies, Development of Government, and Self-Government.

Azizbekova, Pyusta Azizaga kyzy (F)
● Director, Museum of the History of Azerbaijan, Baku. CPSU member.
Elected from NTO No. 199, Azerbaijan SSR. ● Born December 29, 1929;
Azerbaijani; higher education. Professor of history. Corresponding mem-
ber, Azerbaijan SSR Academy of Sciences. Author of several historical
studies of establishment of Communist rule in Azerbaijan. Believed not
to be a supporter of PF of Azerbaijan. Made conservative speech on
nationality issues at CPD (*Pravda*, June 4, 1989). ● Member, Council of
Nationalities Commission on the Development of Culture, Language,
National and Interethnic Traditions, and Preservation of Historical
Heritage.

Barusheva, Lyubov Vasilevna (F)
● Seamstress, Volodarsky Sewn Goods Factory, Baku. Elected from
NTO No. 198, Azerbaijan SSR. ● Born 1941; Russian. Member of USSR
SupSov (1984). ● Member, Council of Nationalities Commission on
Consumer Goods, Trade, and Communal and Household Services for
the Population.

Gadzhiev, Mazakhir Nushiravan ogly
● Leader, team of adjusters, S. M. Kirov Machine-Building Plant, Baku.
CPSU member. Elected from the USSR Trade Unions. ● Member, SupSov
Committee on Public Health.

Ibragimov, Gusein Rustam ogly
● Driller, "Neftyanye Kamni" Maritime Drilling Administration of the

"Twenty-second CPSU Congress" Oil and Gas Administration of the "Kaspmorneftegaz" Production Association, Baku. CPSU member. Elected from the CPSU. ● Born 1951; Azerbaijani. Election platform centered on the need to involve workers in the restructuring process. Says that the declining prestige of the worker and the shortage of young people entering industrial employment are two of today's main problems; notes that even those with higher education from oil and gas institutes end up in commercial, not industrial, jobs (*Pravda*, March 6, 1989). Described tongue in cheek by *Wall Street Journal* (June 7, 1989) as a liberal on grounds he was the only people's deputy from Azerbaijan not wearing a tie. ● Member, SupSov Committee on Legislation, Legality, and Law and Order.

Ismailov, Tofik Kyazim ogly

● General director and chief designer, Space Research Scientific Production Association, Azerbaijan SSR Academy of Sciences, Baku. CPSU member. Elected from NTO No. 215, Azerbaijan SSR. ● Doctor of Technical Sciences. ● Member, SupSov Committee on Economic Reform.

Kafarova, Elmira Mikail kyzy (F)

● Chairman, Presidium, Azerbaijan SSR SupSov, Baku. CPSU member. Elected from NTO No. 224, Azerbaijan SSR. ● Born 1934; Azerbaijani; higher education in philosophy. Appointed to current post in June 1989. Extensive experience in Party and government of Azerbaijan; former Komsomol first secretary, minister of education, minister of foreign affairs and, until recently, deputy chairman, Azerbaijan SSR Council of Ministers. ● Deputy chairman, USSR SupSov Presidium; member, SupSov Committee on International Affairs.

Mamedov, Veli Gusein ogly

● First secretary, Twenty-six Baku Commissars Raikom, Baku. CPSU member. Elected from NTO No. 194, Azerbaijan SSR. ● Outspoken opponent of transfer of Nagorno-Karabakh to Armenia (*Pravda*, May 27, 1989). Criticized MDG, which, he said, threatened to establish a second organizational center in the SupSov and later even a second SupSov (*Moscow News*, No. 32, 1989). ● Member, Council of Nationalities Commission on Nationality Policy and Interethnic Relations.

Namazova, Adilya Avaz kyzy (F)

● Faculty chief, Azerbaijan Medical Institute, Baku. CPSU member. Elected from the Soviet Women's Committee. ● Member, SupSov Committee on Women's Affairs, Family Protection, Motherhood, and Childhood.

Vezirov, Abdul-Rakhman Khalil ogly
● First secretary, CC, CP of Azerbaijan, Baku. CPSU member. Elected from NTO No. 206, Azerbaijan SSR. ● Born 1930; Azerbaijani; higher education. Worked in Party *apparat* before transferring in 1976 to diplomatic service in India, Nepal, and Pakistan. Returned to Party work in May 1988; charged with restoring order in Azerbaijan at height of Nagorno-Karabakh conflict. Purged Party, government, and economic officials in drive against corruption, nepotism and black-marketeering—which he asserted were major causes of the conflict (*Pravda*, October 10, 1988). For his comments on the need to enhance the leading role of the Party and prevent the "slandering" of the past, see *Pravda*, July 21, 1989. ● Member, CPD Constitutional Commission.

From the Belorussian SSR

Bolbasov, Vladimir Sergeevich
● Chief scientific associate and deputy chief of laboratories, Institute of Electronics, Belorussian SSR Academy of Sciences, Minsk. CPSU member. Elected from the All-Union Society of Inventors and Rationalizers. ● Member, SupSov Committee on Science, Public Education, Culture, and Upbringing.

Dubko, Aleksandr Iosifovich
● Chairman, "Progress" Agroindustrial Kolkhoz-Combine, Grodno Raion, Grodno Oblast, Belorussian SSR. CPSU member. Elected from the Council of Kolkhozes. ● Born 1938; Belorussian; higher agricultural education. Has worked in agricultural sector for 30 years. Hero of Socialist Labor. Member of USSR SupSov (1984). ● Member, SupSov Committee on Agrarian Questions and Food.

Golovnev, Vasilii Efimovich
● Aviation technician in a military unit, Bykhov, Mogilev Oblast. CPSU member. Elected from NTO No. 96, Belorussian SSR. ● Born 1954; higher education. ● Member, SupSov Committee on Soviets of People's Deputies, Development of Government, and Self-Government.

Ignatovich, Nikolai Ivanovich
● Investigator for especially important cases under the Office of the Belorussian SSR Prosecutor, Minsk. CPSU member. Elected from NTO No. 65, Belorussian SSR. ● Active in the Belorussian PF. ● Member, CPD Commission to Investigate Materials Linked With the Activity of the USSR's Prosecutor's Office Investigation Group Headed by Telman Gdlyan; member, SupSov Committee on *Glasnost*, Rights, and Appeals of Citizens.

Kiseleva, Valentina Adamovna (F)
● Administrator, "Khimvolokno" Production Association, Grodno. Elected from NTO No. 89, Belorussian SSR. ● Emerged victorious from list of nine candidates, among them the enterprise director at the chemical plant where she has worked for past 12 years. Applauded by some deputies, criticized by others for overstepping her brief, when she spoke at CPD about problems in the Soviet armed forces (*Moscow News*, July 16, 1989). ● Member, CPD Presidium; Council of Nationalities Commission on Social and Economic Development of Union and Autonomous Republics, and Autonomous Oblasts and Okrugs.

Kucheiko, Aleksandr Petrovich
● Leader of a multiskilled team, Construction Administration No. 104, Construction Trust No. 19, Lida, Grodno Oblast. CPSU member. Elected from NTO No. 91, Belorussian SSR. ● Member, SupSov Committee on Construction and Architecture.

Labunov, Vladimir Arkhipovich
● Academician-secretary, Department of Physics, Mathematics, and Information Technology, Belorussian Academy of Sciences, and director, Department of Microelectronics, Minsk Radio Institute. CPSU member. Elected from NTO No. 66, Belorussian SSR. ● Doctor of Technical Sciences. ● Member, SupSov Committee on Science, Public Education, Culture, and Upbringing.

Mateushuk, Zinaida Kondratevna (F)
● Shop chief, "Twenty-fifth CPSU Congress" Electromechanical Plant, Brest. CPSU member. Elected from NTO No. 74, Belorussian SSR. ● Election platform called for three-year paid maternity leave, arguing this would reduce need for preschool day-care centers and make for a healthier young generation. Also focused on ecological issues, opposing

construction of new heavy industrial enterprises in Brest (*Sovetskaya Belorussiya*, April 11, 1989). ● Member, SupSov Committee on Women's Affairs, Family Protection, Motherhood, and Childhood.

Momotova, Tamara Vasilevna (F)
● Deputy chief engineer, Artificial Fur Production Association, Zhlobin, Gomel Oblast. CPSU member. Elected from NTO No. 86, Belorussian SSR. ● Member, Council of Nationalities Commission on Consumer Goods, Trade, and Communal and Household Services for the Population.

Tarazevich, Georgii Stanislavovich
● Chairman, Presidium, Belorussian SSR SupSov, Minsk. CPSU member. Elected from NTO No. 71, Belorussian SSR. ● Born 1937; Belorussian; graduated Lvov Polytechnical Institute. Candidate of Technical Sciences; engineer. Entered Party work 1972. 1983–1985, first secretary, Minsk Gorkom. Appointed to current post in 1985. Member of USSR SupSov (1984). Member, CPSU CC since 1986. Conservative *apparatchik* criticized by progressives in and out of Belorussia for allegedly authorizing violent suppression of demonstration in Minsk in October 1988. Chaired a preliminary (pre-CPD) commission to investigate the April 1989 Tbilisi events; his report was criticized (May 1989) by Georgian SSR Academy of Sciences as "incompetent, incorrect, and unobjective." His chairmanship of the Council of Nationalities Commission on Nationality Policy was opposed by several deputies who noted the slow pace of reform and liberalization in Belorussia. ● Member, CPD Constitutional Commission; deputy chairman, USSR SupSov Presidium; chairman, Council of Nationalities Commission on Nationality Policy and Interethnic Relations.

Yakushkin, Viktor Vladimirovich
● Head of physical education, Secondary Vocational and Technical School No. 147, Vitebsk. CPSU member. Elected from NTO No. 79, Belorussian SSR. ● Member, SupSov Committee on Public Health.

From the Estonian SSR

Aare, Juhan (Aare, Yukhan Iokhannesovich)
● Commentator, Chief Propaganda Editorial Office of Estonian television, Tallinn. CPSU member. Elected from NTO No. 472, Estonian SSR.

● Born 1948; Estonian; higher education. One of Estonia's most popular television journalists; chairman of the Estonian "Green" movement founded in May 1988. ● Member, SupSov Committee on Ecology and the Rational Use of Natural Resources. Member, MDG.

Bronstein, Mikhail (Bronshtein, Mikhail Lazarevich)
● Department head, Tartu State University. CPSU member. Elected from NTO No. 477, Estonian SSR. ● Born 1923. Doctorate in Economics. Member, Estonian SSR Academy of Sciences. Strong proponent of radical economic reform; has written numerous articles calling for republican economic independence and cost accounting (for example, *Kommunist*, No. 5, 1989). Defended striking coal miners, adding that grounds for complaint over health care, labor safety, and food supplies exist not just in mining regions but all over the USSR. "Soviet society," he said, "is now in a situation where it has to pay three or even four times for the past, but nobody wants to pay" (Radio Moscow, July 20, 1989). ● Member, SupSov Committee on Economic Reform. Member, MDG.

Gräzin, Igor (Gryazin, Igor Nikolaevich)
● Chief of department, Institute of Philosophy, Sociology, and Law, Estonian SSR Academy of Sciences, Tartu. CPSU member. Elected from NTO No. 473, Estonian SSR. ● Estonian. Professor of Law. One of the most outspoken leaders of the PF of Estonia and member of its 100-person ruling board. Criticized amendments to Soviet constitution on the grounds they left the regulation of property relations, wages, and price formation to the central authorities and negated the possibility of true economic sovereignty for the republics (*Sovetskaya Estoniya*, November 6, 1988). Charged, on Estonian television in March 1989, that Estonian SupSov was illegitimate under international law because it was installed by an occupation force. Read aloud the secret protocol of the Molotov-Ribbentrop Pact at CPD (Central Television, June 1, 1989). ● Member, CPD Constitutional Commission; Constitutional Oversight Commission; Commission on the Molotov-Ribbentrop Pact; SupSov Committee on Construction and Architecture. Member, MDG.

Hallik, Klara (Khallik, Klara Semenova) (F)
● Leading scientific associate, Institute of Philosophy, Sociology and Law, Estonian SSR Academy of Sciences, Tallinn. CPSU member. Elected from NTO No. 454, Estonian SSR. ● Estonian. Expert on nationality

relations. Lost her job briefly in February 1988 because of her daughter's involvement in "nationalist" activity in Estonia. Called for constitutional reform to transform USSR into a federation of sovereign nation-states enjoying full self-determination (Radio Moscow, June 6, 1989). Member, 100-person ruling board, PF of Estonia. Lost to Georgii Tarazevich in bid to chair Council of Nationalities Commission on Nationality Policy.
● Member, CPD Constitutional Commission; Council of Nationalities Commission on Nationality Policy and Interethnic Relations.

Käbin, Tiit (Kyabin, Tiit Reinkholdovich)
● Scientific secretary, Social Sciences Department of the Estonian SSR Academy of Sciences, Tallinn. CPSU member. Elected from NTO No. 452, Estonian SSR. ● Was 46 years old in June 1989; lawyer. Member, 100-person ruling board of PF of Estonia. Viewed by some as an *apparatchik* masquerading as crusader for Estonian cause. ● Member, CPD Presidium; SupSov Committee on Ecology and the Rational Use of Natural Resources; SupSov Committee on Legislation, Legality, and Law and Order. Member, MDG.

Kahn, Juri (Kakhn, Yurii Kharrievich)
● Senior scientific associate, Institute of Economics, Estonian SSR Academy of Sciences, Tallinn. CPSU member. Elected from the All-Union Komsomol. ● Estonian. Member, Estonian Komsomol CC. Not one of the leading activists of the PF but seen as strong supporter of republican autonomy and sovereignty. ● Member, SupSov Committee on Youth.

Kallas, Siim (Udovich)
● Deputy editor of the newspaper *Rahva Haal*, Tallinn. CPSU member. Elected from NTO No. 474, Estonian SSR. ● Born 1948; Estonian, higher education. Member, 100-person ruling board of PF of Estonia. One of four authors of the original proposal for republican cost accounting (*Edasi*, September 26, 1987). Electoral platform called for *glasnost*, genuine price index, and expanded rights for republican and local government organs (*Izvestia*, March 30, 1989). Denied allegations that Estonian authorities planned any expulsion of non-Estonian population (Radio Moscow, July 25, 1989). ● Member, Council of Nationalities Commission on Social and Economic Development of Union and Autonomous Republics, and Autonomous Oblasts and Okrugs. Member, MDG.

Nugis, Ülo (Nugis, Yulo Iokhannesovich)
● General director, "Estoplast" Production Association, Tallinn. CPSU member. Elected from NTO No. 449, Estonian SSR. ● Estonian. Professional engineer. Activist, PF of Estonia. One of the leaders of the Union of Worker Collectives, a counterforce established in 1988 to the Council of Worker Collectives (an organization of non-Estonians who live and work in the republic). ● Member, Council of Nationalities Commission on Consumer Goods, Trade, and Communal and Household Services for the Population. Member, MDG.

Pupkevich, Tadeus (Pupkevich, Tadeush Karlovich)
● Mobile excavator operator, "Estonslanets" Production Association's "Narvsky" Open Pit, Sillamae. CPSU member. Elected from NTO No. 463, Estonian SSR. ● Belorussian. Has lived in Estonia for 30 years. ● Member, CPD Drafting Commission; SupSov Committee on Ecology and the Rational Use of Natural Resources.

Rüütel, Arnold (Ryuitel, Arnold Fedorovich)
● Chairman, Presidium, Estonian SSR SupSov, Tallinn. CPSU member. Elected from NTO No. 479, Estonian SSR. ● Born May 10, 1928; Estonian; graduated from Estonian Agricultural Institute (Candidate of Agricultural Sciences). Worked as agronomist and teacher. Joined CP relatively late, in 1964; named to Estonian CP CC Buro in 1977. 1977–1979, Estonian CP CC secretary for agriculture; 1979–1983, first deputy chairman, Estonian SSR Council of Ministers. Named to current post in April 1983. Seen as a pro-Estonia *apparatchik* who was instrumental in reestablishing the Estonian flag and who has been purposefully slow to implement legislation drawn up by central authorities but seen in the republic as damaging its interests. ● Deputy chairman, USSR SupSov Presidium; member, CPSU Central Auditing Commission since 1986.

Vooglaid, Ülo (Vooglaid, Yulo Vakhurovich)
● Scientific leader, Rapla Raion Agroindustrial Complex Data Processing and Computer Training Center, Tallinn. CPSU member. Elected from NTO No. 476, Estonian SSR. ● Estonian; sociologist. Member of "New Left" and head of sociological laboratory in 1960s; his innovative work brought him into official disfavor and resulted in closure of the laboratory. Expelled from CPSU in 1975; reinstated in April 1989. Member, 100-person board of PF of Estonia. ● Member, SupSov Committee on Science, Public Education, Culture, and Upbringing. Member, MDG.

From the Georgian SSR

Advadze, Valerian Sergeevich
● Director, Georgian SSR State Planning Committee's Scientific Research Institute on the Economics, Planning and Management of the National Economy, Tbilisi. CPSU member. Elected from NTO No. 163, Georgian SSR. ● Was 58 years old in June 1989; Georgian; higher education. Head of a group of Georgian economists that elaborated a concept of republican cost accounting and self-financing involving a greater degree of republican autonomy than that put forward by the republican authorities (TASS, June 22, 1989). ● Member, Council of Nationalities Commission on Social and Economic Development of Union and Autonomous Republics, and Autonomous Oblasts and Okrugs.

Amonashvili, Shalva Aleksandrovich
● General director, Experimental Scientific Production Pedagogical Association, Georgian SSR Ministry of Public Education, Tbilisi. CPSU member. Elected from the USSR Trade Unions. ● Georgian; educational psychologist; corresponding member, USSR Academy of Pedagogical Sciences. Promised electorate to work for improved maternity benefits (APN, February 6, 1989). In speech to CPD, defended those calling for Georgian sovereignty against charges of extremism; complained that schools had become too authoritarian and called for greater attention to teaching of Georgian history (Central Television, June 2, 1989). See also, "The School Must be Nationalized," *Sovetskaya Estoniya*, July 6, 1989, and cover story, "What Are We Selling?" *Ogonek*, No. 26, 1989.
● Member, SupSov Committee on Science, Public Education, Culture, and Upbringing.

Bakradze, Akakii Viktorovich
● Artistic leader, K. Mardzhanishvili State Academic Theater, Tbilisi. Elected from NTO No. 167, Georgian SSR. ● Member, Council of Nationalities Commission on Development of Culture, Language, National and Interethnic Traditions, and Preservation of Historical Heritage.

Dikhtyar, Anatolii Dmitrievich
● Leader of a multiskilled team, "Tbilgorstroi" Association's No. 5 Housing Construction Combine, Tbilisi. CPSU member. Elected from NTO No. 165, Georgian SSR. ● Member, SupSov Committee on Construction and Architecture.

Guguchiya, Dzhoto Iosifovich
● Chairman, Karl Marx Kolkhoz, Zugdidsky Raion, Georgian SSR. CPSU member. Elected from the Council of Kolkhozes. ● Member, SupSov Committee on Agrarian Questions and Food.

Gumbaridze, Givi Grigorevich
● First secretary, CC, CP of Georgia, Tbilisi. CPSU member. Elected from NTO No. 175, Georgian SSR. ● Born 1945; Georgian; graduate of Tbilisi State University. Worked in apparatus of Georgian CP CC until December 1988, when appointed chairman of republican KGB. In April 1989, promoted to head republican Party organization when Dzhumber Patiashvili resigned following violent suppression by police and army of demonstrations in Tbilisi. At CPD, spoke in passionate defense of the demonstrators and denounced the military commander responsible for the massacre; called for the establishment of legal basis for political and economic sovereignty for Georgia (Central Television, June 8, 1989). Appealed on republican television for calm during ethnic violence in Abkhazia in July 1989. ● Member, CPD Constitutional Commission.

Kurashvili, Zeinab Givievna (F)
● Sewing machine operator, "Gldani" Knitwear Production Association, Tbilisi. CPSU member. Elected from NTO No. 162, Georgian SSR. ● Member, CPD Presidium; Council of Nationalities Commission on Consumer Goods, Trade, and Communal and Household Services for the Population.

Menteshashvili, Tengiz Nikolaevich
● Secretary, Presidium, USSR SupSov. CPSU member. Elected from NTO No. 180, Georgian SSR. ● Born 1928; Georgian; engineer. Close ties to Eduard Shevardnadze; was second secretary of the Georgian Komsomol CC in 1958 when Shevardnadze was first secretary. His career advanced rapidly after Shevardnadze's appointment in 1972 as republican Party boss. 1973, first secretary, Rustavi Gorkom; 1976, first secretary, Tbilisi Gorkom. Appointed to current post in 1982. Candidate member, CPSU CC since 1986. Member of USSR SupSov (1984).

Spanderashvili, Tamaz Mikhailovich
● Steel worker, Rustavi Metallurgical Plant, Rustavi. CPSU member. Elected from NTO No. 182, Georgian SSR. ● Georgian.

Stepnadze, Telman Sergeevich
- Team leader, Alsky Viticultural Sovkhoz, Khashursky Raion. CPSU member. Elected from NTO No. 169, Georgian SSR. ● Member, SupSov Committee on Veterans and Invalids.

Tabukashvili, Revaz Shalvovich
- Leader, "Gruziyafilm" Movie Studio Screenplay Association, Tbilisi. CPSU member. Elected from NTO No. 170, Georgian SSR. ● Member, Council of Nationalities Commission on Nationality Policy and Interethnic Relations.

From the Kazakh SSR

Akhmetova, Rushangul Sunurovna (F)
- Teacher, Ch. Valikhanova Secondary School, Kainazar, Enbekshi-kazakhsky Raion, Alma-Ata Oblast. Elected from NTO No. 131, Kazakh SSR. ● Member, SupSov Committee on Science, Public Education, Culture, and Upbringing.

Auelbekov, Erkin Nurzhanovich
- First secretary, Kzyl-Orda Obkom. CPSU member. Elected from NTO No. 144, Kazakh SSR. ● Born 1930; Kazakh; agronomist with higher education. Member, CPSU CC since 1976; worked in Party and government posts since 1961. Member of USSR SupSov (1984). For statement on efforts to implement *perestroika* in his oblast, see *Pravda*, March 1, 1988. ● Chairman, Council of Nationalities Commission for the Study of the Sociopolitical Situation in Moldavia; member, Council of Nationalities Commission on Nationality Policy and Interethnic Relations.

Dzhumatova, Menslu Duisenbaevna (F)
- Chief physician, Dzhambul Rural District Hospital, Chapaevsky Raion, Uralsk Oblast, Kazakh SSR. Elected from the USSR Trade Unions.
- Member, SupSov Committee on Public Health.

Klishchuk, Petr Martynovich
- Team leader, "Salkynkolsky" Sovkhoz, Chistopolsky Raion, Kokchetav Oblast. CPSU member. Elected from NTO No. 145, Kazakh SSR.
- Member, SupSov Committee on Veterans and Invalids.

Kozhakhmetov, Ibraimzhan
● Chairman, Kirov Kolkhoz, Panfilovsky Raion, Taldy-Kurgan Oblast, Kazakh SSR. CPSU member. Elected from the Council of Kolkhozes.
● Member, CPD Presidium; Council of Nationalities Commission on Social and Economic Development of Union and Autonomous Republics, and Autonomous Oblasts and Okrugs.

Medeubekov, Kiilybai Usenovich
● Chairman, Presidium, Eastern Branch, VASKhNIL, Alma-Ata. CPSU member. Elected from VASKhNIL. ● Member, SupSov Committee on Agrarian Questions and Food.

Rakhmadiev, Erkegali
● Composer; first secretary, Kazakhstan Composers' Union Board, Alma-Ata. CPSU member. Elected from NTO No. 134, Kazakh SSR.
● Wrote an opera based on Brezhnev's autobiographical *Tselina* (Virgin Lands) in 1981. ● Member, Council of Nationalities Commission on Development of Culture, Language, National and Interethnic Traditions, and Preservation of Historical Heritage.

Romazanov, Kabdulla Zakiryanovich
● Steelworker, Metallurgical Combine, Temirtau, Karaganda Oblast, Kazakh SSR. CPSU member. Elected from the CPSU. ● Born 1947; Kazakh. Has worked in current position since 1978. Member, CPSU CAC since 1986. ● Member, SupSov Committee on Ecology and the Rational Use of Natural Resources.

Shtoik, Garri Gvidovich
● Director, East Kazakhstan Copper and Chemical Combine, "Kazpoli-metall" Production Association, Ust-Talovka Settlement, Shemonaikhin-sky Raion, East Kazakhstan Oblast, Kazakh SSR. CPSU member. Elected from the CPSU. ● Born 1939. ● Member, SupSov Committee on Economic Reform.

Veiser, Ledzher Marovich
● Secretary, Komsomol Committee, Masanchi Secondary School, Kurdai-sky Raion, Dzhambul Oblast, Kazakh SSR. CPSU member. Elected from the Komsomol. ● Was 26 in May 1989. Afghan veteran; teacher of history and geography. ● Member, SupSov Committee on Soviets of People's Deputies, Development of Government, and Self-Government.

Vidiker, Vladimir Ivanovich
● Director, "Suvorovsky" Sovkhoz, Irtyshsky Raion, Pavlodar Oblast. CPSU member. Elected from NTO No. 160, Kazakh SSR. ● Member, SupSov Committee on Veterans and Invalids.

From the Kirgiz SSR

Aitmatov, Chingiz
● Chairman, Kirgiz SSR Writers' Union Board; chief editor, journal *Inostrannaya literatura*. CPSU member. Elected from the CPSU.
● Born 1928; Kirgiz; son of victim of Stalin purges; higher education. Member of USSR SupSov (1984). Influential popular novelist whose works have broached sensitive moral questions such as religion, nationality relations, the Stalin terror, environmental protection, and drug abuse. In 1986, founded Issyk-Kul Cultural Forum, which brought together leading cultural figures from all over the world. At CPD, came out strongly in favor of preservation of minority languages and autonomy of small nations; proposed work in agricultural sector as alternative to military service; held up Western democracies such as Norway, Spain, and Switzerland as examples for Soviet emulation (Central Television, June 2, 1989). ● Member, CPD Presidium; CPD Drafting Commission; chairman, CPD Commission Examining the Molotov-Ribbentrop Pact; member, USSR SupSov Presidium; chairman, Council of Nationalities Commission on the Development of Culture, Language, National and Interethnic Traditions, and Preservation of Historical Heritage.

Akaev, Askar
● President, Kirgiz SSR Academy of Sciences, Frunze. CPSU member. Elected from NTO No. 339, Kirgiz SSR. ● Born 1944; Kirgiz; higher education. Member, CC, CP of Kirgizia. ● Member, CPD Constitutional Oversight Commission; SupSov Committee on Economic Reform.

Akmatalieva, Urukan Kalilovna (F)
● Silk reeler, All-Union Komsomol Silk Industrial and Trade Association, Osh. CPSU member. Elected from NTO No. 340, Kirgiz SSR.
● Member, SupSov Committee on Legislation, Legality and Law and Order.

Akmatov, Tashtanbek
• Chairman, Presidium, Kirgiz SSR SupSov, Frunze. CPSU member. Elected from NTO No. 329, Kirgiz SSR. • Born 1938; Kirgiz; higher education. Worked as shepherd until his unexpected appointment in 1987 as president of Kirgizia. Member of USSR SupSov (1984). • Deputy chairman, USSR SupSov Presidium.

Barabanov, Vyacheslav Ivanovich
• Head of sheep breeding unit, "Kommunizm" Kolkhoz, Dzheti-Oguzsky Raion, Issyk-Kul Oblast. CPSU member. Elected from NTO No. 341, Kirgiz SSR. • Member, SupSov Committee on Agrarian Questions and Food.

Beishekeeva, Zaina (F)
• Senior shepherd, Special State Farm, Dzhety-Oguz Raion, Issyk-Kul Oblast, Kirgiz SSR. CPSU member. Elected from the CPSU. • Born 1955. Member, CPSU CAC since 1986. "One of the best shepherds in Kirgizia" (*Agitator*, November 1986). • Member, SupSov Committee on Youth.

Isakov, Ismanali Ismailovich
• Face worker, Khaidarkan Mercury Combine, Frunze Raion, Osh Oblast. CPSU member. Elected from NTO No. 352, Kirgiz SSR. • Member, SupSov Committee on Ecology and the Rational Use of Natural Resources.

Kiselev, Gennadii Nikolaevich
• Second secretary, CC, CP of Kirgizia, Frunze. CPSU member. Elected from NTO No. 327, Kirgiz SSR. • Born 1936; Russian; higher education in economics. Candidate member, CPSU CC since 1986. Served 25 years in Magadan Party organization; transferred to Moscow in 1985 as CPSU CC inspector. No experience in Kirgizia before December 1985. • Member, USSR SupSov Presidium; chairman, Council of Nationalities Commission on Consumer Goods, Trade, and Communal and Household Services for the Population; chairman, Council of Nationalities Commission on Soviet Germans.

Kuldyshev, Mamidali Sagimbekovich
• Leader, Komsomol team, "Tash-Kumyrstroi" Trust's Mobile Mechanized Column No. 370, Tash-Kumyr. Elected from NTO No. 346, Kirgiz SSR. • Member, SupSov Committee on Construction and Agriculture.

Orozova, Umtul Sheisheevna (F)
● Chairman, Kirgiz SSR State Committee for Television and Radio Broadcasting, Frunze. Elected from the Soviet Women's Committee. ● Born 1939; graduated from Kirgiz State University and State University for Theatrical Arts. Formerly chief, Cultural Department, Kirgiz CP CC.
● Member, SupSov Committee on International Affairs.

Zanokha, Aleksandr Ivanovich
● Chairman, Lenin Kolkhoz, Alamedinsky Raion. CPSU member. Elected from NTO No 326, Kirgiz SSR.

From the Latvian SSR

Bišers, Ilmārs (Bisher, Ilmar Olertovich)
● Professor, P. Stučka Latvian State University, Riga. CPSU member. Elected from NTO No. 317, Latvian SSR. ● Was 59 in June 1989; Latvian. Lawyer with higher education. Member, PF of Latvia. ● Deputy chairman, Council of Nationalities, USSR SupSov; member, CPD Constitutional Commission; CPD Commission to Investigate Materials Linked with the Activity of the USSR's Prosecutor's Office Investigation Group Headed by Telman Gdlyan.

Klibiķe, Valentīna (Klibik, Valentina Sergeevna) (F)
● CPSU member. Elected from the Soviet Women's Committee. ● Born 1930; Latvian; higher education. Conservative. Extensive experience in Latvian CP and government. Resigned as secretary, Presidium, Latvian SSR SupSov to serve in USSR SupSov. ● Secretary, SupSov Committee on Women's Affairs, Family Protection, Motherhood, and Childhood.

Kostenetskaya, Marina Grigorevna (F)
● Writer; Riga. Elected from NTO No. 312, Latvian SSR ● Russian. Progressive; prolific author on social topics. Member, PF of Latvia.
● Member, SupSov Committee on Veterans and Invalids.

Kukaine, Rita (Kukain, Rita Aleksandrovna) (F)
● Director, A. Kirhensteins Institute of Microbiology of the Latvian SSR Academy of Sciences, Riga. CPSU member. Elected from NTO No. 320, Latvian SSR.● Born 1922; Latvian; Doctor of Medical Sciences. Little prior

experience in Party or government. Member of USSR SupSov (1984).
Member, PF of Latvia. ● Member, SupSov Committee on Ecology and
the Rational Use of Natural Resources.

Lucāns, Jānis (Lutsans, Yanis Petrovich)
● Chairman, "Komunars" Kolkhoz-Agrocombine, Limbazi Raion. CPSU
member. Elected from NTO No. 308, Latvian SSR. ● Latvian; graduate,
Latvian Agricultural Academy. Member, PF of Latvia. Active proponent
of agricultural reform. ● Member, Council of Nationalities Commission
on Social and Economic Development of Union and Autonomous
Republics, and Autonomous Oblasts and Okrugs.

Neilands, Nikolajs (Neiland, Nikolai Vasilevich)
● Deputy foreign minister, Latvian SSR. CPSU member. Elected
from NTO No. 292, Riga. ● Latvian. Implicated in charges of espionage
in former post as head of the APN bureau in Stockholm. Member,
PF of Latvia. ● Member, CPD Commission on the Molotov-Ribbentrop
Pact.

Ņukša, Konstantīns (Nyuksha, Konstantin Ivanovich)
● Fitter and tool maker, "Rizhsky Elektormashinostroitelnyi Zavod"
Production Association, Riga. CPSU member. Elected from the CPSU.
● Born 1938; Latvian. Conservative. ● Member, Council of Nationalities
Commission on Consumer Goods, Trade, and Communal and House-
hold Services for the Population.

Peters, Jānis (Peters, Yanis Yanovich)
● Writer; chairman, Latvian SSR Writers' Association Board, Riga. CPSU
member. Elected from NTO No. 299, Latvian SSR. ● Born 1939; Latvian.
Prolific poet who chaired the founding congress of the PF of Latvia,
October 1988. Early spokesman for republican sovereignty (*Pravda*,
September 16, 1987). Called at CPD for independence and sovereignty
for union republics: "only genuinely independent states with some
limitation on their independence, as can be observed in all federal
unions, can now lead us out of our political, economic, ecological and
national crisis . . ." (Central Television, June 2, 1989). ● Member, Council
of Nationalities Commission on Development of Culture, Language,
National and Interethnic Traditions, and Preservation of Historical
Heritage.

Rubiks, Alfreds (Petrovich)
● Chairman, Riga Gorispolkom. CPSU member. Elected from NTO No. 290, Latvian SSR. ● Born 1935; Latvian; graduated Riga Polytechnical Institute and Higher Party School. Worked as engineer before switching to Komsomol and Party work. 1982–1984, Latvian SSR minister of light industry. Named to current post in May 1984. Has since acquired reputation as staunch Gorbachev supporter. Took tough line toward nationalist demonstrations in Riga in 1987, organizing a counter-demonstration in response to an unofficial demonstration marking anniversary of loss of Baltic independence; indicated that authorities would stop any "manifestation of nationalist or anti-Soviet sentiment" (AP, November 18, 1987). Called for tax revenue to go to local soviets instead of central authorities (*Izvestia*, June 28, 1989). Becoming steadily less popular in own republic. ● Member, SupSov Committee on Soviets of People's Deputies, Development of Government, and Self-Government.

Shamikhin, Albert Mikhailovich
● Responsible organizer, CC, Trade Union of Automotive and Agricultural Machine-Building Workers, Riga. CPSU member. Elected from the USSR Trade Unions. ● Member, Council of Nationalities Commission on Social and Economic Development of Union and Autonomous Republics, and Autonomous Oblasts and Okrugs.

Vulfsons, Mavriks (Vulfson, Mavrik Germanovich)
● Senior lecturer, Social Sciences Department, Latvian Academy of Arts, Riga. CPSU member. Elected from NTO No. 296, Latvian SSR. ● Latvian-Jewish. Political commentator for Latvian television. At public rally in July 1988 said Latvia's absorption into the USSR in 1940 was not a revolution, but the installation of a Stalinist dictatorship. Member, PF of Latvia; recent convert to the progressives. ● Member, CPD Commission on Molotov-Ribbentrop Pact; SupSov Committee on International Affairs.

From the Lithuanian SSR

Bičkauskas, Egidijus (Bichkauskas, Egidiyus Vitautovich)
● Investigator for especially important cases, Lithuanian SSR Prosecutor's Office, Vilnius. CPSU member. Elected from NTO No. 254, Lithuanian SSR. ● Born 1955; Lithuanian. In early 1980s, was involved in the

investigation of a prominent Lithuanian Catholic priest. A recent convert to the progressive wing in Lithuania whose candidacy to the CPD was supported by Sajudis. At CPD, raised question of Molotov-Ribbentrop Pact (Central Television, May 29, 1989). ● Deputy chairman, CPD Commission to Investigate Materials Linked with the Activity of the USSR's Prosecutor's Office Investigation Group Headed by Telman Gdlyan; member, SupSov Committee on Legislation, Legality, and Law and Order.

Genzelis, Bronius (Genzyalis, Bronislavas Konstantinovich)
● Professor, V. Kapsukas Vilnius State University. CPSU member. Elected from NTO No. 243, Lithuanian SSR. ● Born February 16, 1934; Lithuanian. Doctor of Philosophy. Party Secretary, Vilnius University. Member, Sajudis inner council. ● Member, Council of Nationalities Commission on Nationality Policy and Interethnic Relations. Member, MDG.

Gudaitis, Romas (Vitautovich)
● Writer, literary consultant to the Lithuanian SSR Writers' Union, Vilnius. CPSU member. Elected from NTO No. 235, Lithuanian SSR.
● Born December 8, 1941; Estonian; higher education. Member, Sajudis inner council. Formerly worked in Lithuanian film industry. Spoke at CPD in support of republican sovereignty, saying: "No institution may set itself above the interests of the people of my Lithuania, to say nothing of suspending the laws of a sovereign republic!" (Central Television, June 8, 1989).

Kudarauskas, Sigitas (Yuozovich)
● Chief, Department of Electrotechnical Disciplines, Kaunas Polytechnical Institute's Klaipeda faculties. CPSU member. Elected from NTO No. 241, Lithuanian SSR. ● Born January 1, 1936; Lithuanian; Doctorate in Electrical Engineering. Member, Sajudis. ● Member, CPD Secretariat; SupSov Committee on International Affairs.

Kupliauskienė, Juratė (Kuplyauskene, Yurate Iono) (F)
● Chairman, student trade union committee, Engineering-Construction Institute, Vilnius. CPSU member. Elected from NTO No. 226, Lithuanian SSR. ● Born 1964; Lithuanian. Member, Sajudis. ● Member, SupSov Committee on Women's Affairs, Family Protection, Motherhood, and Childhood.

Medvedev, Nikolai Nikolaevich
● Sector chief, Scientific Research Institute of Radio Measuring Equipment, Kaunas. CPSU member. Elected from NTO No. 237, Lithuanian SSR. ● Born 1933; Russian. Member, Sajudis Sejm. Won over 60 percent of the vote in election to CPD. Rebutted attacks by other deputies on Baltic delegations at CPD (Central Television, June 2, 1989). ● Member, Council of Nationalities Commission on Nationality Policy and Interethnic Relations. Member, MDG.

Motieka, Kazimieras (Moteka, Kazimir Vladislavovich)
● Lawyer, First Vilnius Legal Consultation Office. Elected from NTO No. 232, Lithuanian SSR. ● Born 1929; Lithuanian. Member, Sajudis inner council. Former CPSU member who quit the Party during CPD election campaign; for his explanation, see *Vozrozhdenie*, February 12, 1989. Called on Lithuanian SSR Council of Ministers to take action over deforestation of areas of Lithuania used as military bases (Radio Vilnius, July 7, 1989). ● Member, CPD Commission on the Molotov-Ribbentrop Pact; SupSov Committee on Legislation, Legality, and Law and Order.

Olekas, Juozas (Olekas, Youza Youzovich)
● Senior scientific associate, Laboratory of Problematic Microsurgery, V. Kapsukas Vilnius State University. Elected from NTO No. 233, Lithuanian SSR. ● Born 1955; Lithuanian. Member, Sajudis Sejm. Previously unknown doctor backed by Sajudis in CPD elections. Won 71 percent of the vote and defeated the chairman of the Lithuanian SupSov. ● Member, SupSov Committee on Public Health.

Uoka, Kazimieras (Uoko, Kazimiras Kosto)
● Secretary, Sajudis; bulldozer driver, "Kauno Statiba" Construction and Installation Trust's No. 14 Mechanized Earth Work Administration, Kaunas. CPSU member. Elected from NTO No. 238, Lithuanian SSR. ● Born 1951; Lithuanian; Candidate of History. Member, Sajudis inner council. Grass-roots workers' spokesman. Organizer of conference, held in Moscow in July 1989, of representatives of emergent workers' clubs and unofficial unions; said official trade unions were out of touch with workers' interests (*Guardian*, July 10, 1989). Told SupSov during July 1989 miners' strikes that workers had no faith in the official unions (TASS, July 24, 1989). Initiated the Lithuanian Workers' Association, a group advocating independent labor unions, private property, and improved social welfare (*Washington Post*, August 6, 1989).

Vilkas, Edvardas (Vilkas, Eduardas Iono)
● Chief scientific secretary, Lithuanian SSR Academy of Sciences, and director of its Institute of Economics, Vilnius. CPSU member. Elected from NTO No. 225, Lithuanian SSR. ● Born October 3, 1935; Lithuanian. Doctorate in Mathematical Economics. Supporter of Sajudis. ● Member, USSR SupSov Presidium; chairman, Council of Nationalities Commission on Social and Economic Development of Union and Autonomous Republics, and Autonomous Oblasts and Okrugs.

Zaleckas, Kęstutis (Zaletskas, Kyastutis Vatslavovich)
● First secretary, Vilnius Gorkom. CPSU member. Elected from NTO No. 229, Lithuanian SSR. ● Born September 19, 1943; Lithuanian; graduated from Azerbaijan Institute of Oil and Chemistry and Leningrad Higher Party School. Extensive experience in Party and government *apparat* in Lithuania. Candidate member, Lithuanian CP Buro since 1988. Defeated a Sajudis candidate in election to CPD.

From the Moldavian SSR

Chiriac, Nelia (Kiriyak, Nellya Pavlovna) (F)
● Secretary, Presidium, Moldavian SSR SupSov, Kishinev. CPSU member. Elected from the Soviet Women's Committee. ● Born 1935; Moldavian; higher technical and Party education. Member, CC, CP of Moldavia. Extensive Party and government experience in Moldavia. Viewed as a weathervane—once a staunch Brezhnevite who is now a crusader for *perestroika*. Heaped praise upon Gorbachev and Lukyanov in CPD speech, for which she was rebuked by Moldavian progressive, Mihai Cimpoi, who said Chiriac's "praise-singing and eulogies" were not helpful to the democratization process (Central Television, May 29, 1989). ● Member, SupSov Committee on Soviets of People's Deputies, Development of Government, and Self-Government.

Cimpoi, Mihai (Chimpoi, Mikhail Ilich)
● Writer; secretary, Moldavian SSR Writers' Union Board, Kishinev. Elected from NTO No. 258, Moldavian SSR. ● Moldavian. Literary historian of international repute who was elected to CPD with support of unofficial movements in Moldavia. In CPD speech, called for suspension of decree of Presidium of USSR SupSov dated April 8, 1989, which

provided for the punishment of those "discrediting" public institutions and officials; criticized SupSov July 1988 decrees that empowered special troops to deal with unauthorized rallies and demonstrations; called for resolution on the statehood and function of national languages (Radio Moscow, May 29, 1989). Is, together with with Ion Druță, the most progressive and reformist of the Moldavian deputies in USSR SupSov. ● Member, Council of Nationalities Commission on Development of Culture, Language, National and Interethnic Traditions, and Preservation of Historical Heritage.

Doga, Eugeniu (Doga, Evgenii Dmitrievich)
● Composer; first deputy chairman, Moldavian SSR Composers' Union Board, Kishinev. CPSU member. Elected from NTO No. 288, Moldavian SSR. ● Moldavian. Not affiliated with Moldavia's unofficial movements but won election to CPD with their support. ● Member, SupSov Committee on Science, Public Education, Culture, and Upbringing.

Druță, Ion (Drutse, Ion Panteleevich)
● Writer, Moscow. CPSU member. Elected from NTO No. 265, Moldavian SSR. ● Moldavian; doyen of republican literature; elected with support of Moldavian unofficial groups. Fell out of favor with republican authorities in the 1970s because his writings emphasized Moldavian culture and criticized influx of other nationalities into the republic. Electoral platform called for churches that had been closed or "misappropriated" by the state to be returned to the community and for monasteries to be reopened; donated own money for church restoration and urged voters to be guided by God in their election choice (*Literatura și arta*, March 23, 1989). In hard-hitting speech at CPD, asked Gorbachev to explain discrepancy between the USSR's international rhetoric that emphasizes the peaceful resolution of conflict and its domestic reliance on the use of force (Radio Moscow, June 1, 1989).

Kanarovskaya, Anna Matveevna (F)
● Deputy director and chief economist, Dzerzhinsky Sovkhoz-Plant, Dubossarsky Raion. CPSU member. Elected from NTO No. 266, Moldavian SSR. ● Ukrainian. Elected from Russified area of Moldavia. Shares opinions on language issue with the conservative "Interfront" movement (uniting non-Moldavians living in the republic). Defeated unpopular president of the Moldavian Academy of Sciences, Aleksandr Zhuchenko, in election to CPD. (Zhuchenko had been targeted for

defeat by unofficial groups and the "Greens" because of his alleged involvement in chemical and biological pollution in Moldavia.)
● Member, Council of Nationalities Commission on Consumer Goods, Trade, and Communal and Household Services to the Population.

Kostishin, Nikolai Anatolevich
● Metalworker and assembler, "Pribor" Plant, Bendery. Elected from NTO No. 263, Moldavian SSR. ● After CPD met, complained that too many deputies spoke for the sake of appearing on television and said that, while many proposals were raised about what should be done, few deputies offered practical solutions. Restated the conservative argument that democracy and discipline are indivisible (*Izvestia*, June 12, 1989).
● Member, SupSov Committee on International Affairs.

Moşneaga, Timofei (Moshnyaga, Timofei Vasilevich)
● Chief physician, Republic Clinical Hospital, Kishinev. CPSU member. Elected from NTO No. 257, Moldavian SSR. ● Moldavian. At SupSov session, critical of the appointment of republican procurators by Moscow instead of by the republics (Radio Moscow, June 7, 1989). ● Member, SupSov Committee on International Affairs.

Palagnyuk, Boris Timofeevich
● Director, "Sixtieth Anniversary of the USSR" Pedigree Poultry Breeding Sovkhoz, Rybnitsky Raion. CPSU member. Elected from NTO No. 278, Moldavian SSR. ● Ukrainian. Elected from heavily Russified area of Moldavia. Signed petitions protesting proposed return of Moldavian language to Latin script. In speech to SupSov Council of Nationalities, criticized the language movements in non-Russian republics and proposed giving Russian the status of a state language (*Izvestia*, June 8, 1989).

Pashaly, Mikhail Konstantinovich
● Chairman, Agroindustrial Association, Chadyr-Lunga Raion. CPSU member. Elected from NTO No. 287, Moldavian SSR. ● Gagauz. Elected from a non-Moldavian area of the republic.

Platon, Semen Ivanovich
● Chairman, Kagul Gorispolkom. CPSU member. Elected from NTO No. 268, Moldavian SSR. ● Moldavian. ● Member, CPD Constitutional Commission; CPD Drafting Commission; SupSov Committee on Construction and Architecture.

Zamaneagra, Mihai (Zamanyagra, Mikhail Fedorovich)
● Leader of team of drivers, "Beltsytrans" Production Association, Beltsy, Moldavian SSR. Elected from the USSR Trade Unions.
● Moldavian. Says that ecological and economic problems should be priority items on SupSov agenda; thinks language issues are not first-order problems. Believes money is wasted on useless, harmful projects. Disappointed that CPD deputies were heavy on eloquent phrases, but light on constructive proposals (*Sovetskaya Moldaviya*, June 7, 1989).

From the Tajik SSR

Britvin, Nikolai Vasilevich
● Lieutenant general; chief, Political Directorate, USSR KGB Border Troops. CPSU member. Elected from NTO No. 375, Tajik SSR. ● For statement on indispensable functions of Soviet border guards, see TASS, May 26, 1989; refutes claims of "bourgeois propaganda," asserting that three times more people try to enter the USSR illegally than try to flee it. ● Member, SupSov Committee on Defense and State Security.

Fatullaev, Mirbako
● Deputy chief physician, Central Raion Hospital, Ura-Tyube. CPSU member. Elected from NTO No. 381, Tajik SSR. ● Member, SupSov Committee on Public Health.

Gulova, Zulaikho Sokhibnazarovna (F)
● Field crop cultivation team leader, "Twenty-second Party Congress" Kolkhoz, Ordzhonikidzeabad Raion, Tajik SSR. CPSU member. Elected from the CPSU. ● Born 1949. Member, CPSU CAC since 1986. ● Member, Council of Nationalities Commission on Social and Economic Development of Union and Autonomous Republics, and Autonomous Oblasts and Okrugs.

Khusanbaev, Mutallim Abdumuminovich
● Caster and molder, "Leninabadselmash" Plant, Kushtegirman Kishlak, Nausky Raion. Elected from NTO No. 376, Tajik SSR. ● Member, SupSov Committee on Veterans and Invalids.

Kodyrov, Barakatulo Kamarovich
● Senior shepherd, Khasan Sovkhoz, Varmonik, Leninsky Raion. CPSU member. Elected from NTO No. 373, Tajik SSR. ● Member, SupSov Committee on Agrarian Questions and Food.

Manko, Nikolai Mikhailovich
● Assembly worker, Construction and Assembly Administration No. 3, "Dushanbezhilstroi" Planning and Construction Administration, Dushanbe. CPSU member. Elected from NTO No. 355, Tajik SSR. ● Member, SupSov Committee on Construction and Architecture.

Odzhiev, Rizoali Kadamshoevich
● Deputy chairman, "Internatsionalist" Cooperative Association, Dushanbe. Elected from the All-Union Komsomol. ● Was 27 in May 1989. Veteran of Afghan war who shared his cooperative's first earnings with the family of soldier killed in Afghanistan. Ardent supporter of cooperative movement (*Pravda,* June 12, 1989). ● Member, CPD Commission to Investigate the April 1989 Events in Tbilisi; Council of Nationalities Commission on Nationality Policy and Interethnic Relations.

Pallaev, Gaibnazar
● Chairman, Presidium, Tajik SSR SupSov, Dushanbe. CPSU member. Elected from NTO No. 358, Tajik SSR. ● Born 1929; Tajik; graduated Tajik Agricultural Institute. Worked as agronomist before entering Party work in Tajikistan. Appointed to current post in February 1984. Member, CPSU CAC since 1986. Member of USSR SupSov (1984). ● Member, CPD Drafting Commission; deputy chairman, USSR SupSov Presidium.

Rakhimova, Bikhodzhal Fatkhitdinovna (F)
● Party secretary for ideology, Leninabad Obkom, Tajik SSR. CPSU member. Elected from the Soviet Women's Committee. ● Election platform focused on international and patriotic education of upcoming generation (*Kommunist Tadzhikistana,* March 24, 1989). Spoke at CPD on social issues; claimed infant mortality in Tajikistan was twice the national average and called on the SupSov to establish a state fund to equalize socioeconomic conditions in the regions and republics. Stated women had "lost" in the SupSov elections because there were only half as many women in the reconstituted SupSov as in the previous one (*Izvestia,* June 8, 1989). ● Member, SupSov Committee on Women's Affairs, Family Protection, Motherhood, and Childhood.

Safarov, Bozorali Solikhovich
● Shift engineer, Aviation Technology Base, Kulyab Airport. Candidate member CPSU. Elected from NTO No. 369, Tajik SSR. ● Member, SupSov Committee on *Glasnost*, Rights, and Appeals of Citizens.

Safieva, Gulrukhsor (F)
● Poet; chairman, Tajik SSR Branch of the Soviet Cultural Foundation, Dushanbe. CPSU member. Elected from the Soviet Cultural Foundation.
● Tajik; poet who writes in Tajik and Russian. Pre-CPD statement expresses concern about women's issues (*Pravda*, May 22, 1989). Queried Ryzhkov about the USSR's "arrogant obsession with economic projects" like the Rogun hydroelectric station in Tajikistan (Central Television, June 7, 1989). ● Member, SupSov Committee on International Affairs.

From the Turkmen SSR

Akmamedov, Geldy Mamedmuradovich
● Master baker, No. 1 Bakery of the "Ashkhabadkhleb" Production Association, Ashkhabad. CPSU member. Elected from NTO No. 418, Turkmen SSR. ● Member, Council of Nationalities Commission on Consumer Goods, Trade, and Communal and Household Services to the Population.

Allayarov, Redzhapbai Allayarovich
● Chairman, Kalinin Kolkhoz, Voroshilov Settlement, Tashauz Raion, Tashauz Oblast. CPSU member. Elected from NTO No. 443, Turkmen SSR. ● For pre-election statement declaring intention of focusing on problems of Turkmenia, see *Pravda*, May 19, 1989. ● Member, SupSov Committee on Agrarian Questions and Food.

Annamukhamedov, Atakhodzhamengli
● Deputy commander, First Flight Squadron, Turkmen Civil Aviation Administration, Ashkhabad. CPSU member. Elected from NTO No. 417, Turkmen SSR. ● Member, Council of Nationalities Commission on Nationality Policy and Interethnic Relations.

Atdaev, Khodzhamukhamed
● Blacksmith, "Fiftieth Anniversary of the USSR" Petroleum Machine

Building Plant, Ashkhabad. CPSU member. Elected from NTO No. 420, Turkmen SSR. ● Member, Council of Nationalities Commission on Social and Economic Development of Union and Autonomous Republics, and Autonomous Oblasts and Okrugs.

Baleshev, Nikolai Fedorovich
● First secretary, Ashkhabad Gorkom. CPSU member. Elected from NTO No. 419, Turkmen SSR. ● Member, SupSov Committee on Soviets of People's Deputies, Development of Government, and Self-Government.

Bazarova, Roza Atamuradovna (F)
● Chairman, Presidium, Turkmen SSR SupSov, Ashkhabad. CPSU member. Elected from NTO No. 436, Turkmen SSR. ● Born July 1933. Doctor of History. Formerly deputy prime minister and minister of foreign affairs of Turkmenia. Coauthored two-volume history of Soviet Turkmenistan. Advocates granting real power to local soviets to plan the socioeconomic development of their regions (APN, August 23, 1988). ● Member, CPD Drafting Commission; deputy chairman, USSR SupSov Presidium.

Gundogdyev, Yazgeldi Potaevich
● CPSU member, Ashkhabad. Elected from NTO No. 424, Turkmen SSR. ● Former first secretary, Turkmen Komsomol CC. ● Member, SupSov Committee on Youth.

Ishanov, Khekim
● Chief engineer, "Turkmenneft" Production Association, Nebit-Dag. CPSU member. Elected from NTO No. 439, Turkmen SSR. Member, CPD Presidium.

Kurbanova, Amangozel (F)
● Carpet maker, "Turkmenkover" Production Association, Ashkhabad. Elected from the Soviet Women's Committee. ● Claims women are bought and sold in Central Asia (*Pravda*, October 27, 1988). ● Member, SupSov Committee on Women's Affairs, Family Protection, Motherhood, and Childhood.

Meleev, Kaka
● Chief agronomist, "Leningrad" Kolkhoz, Takhtinsky Raion, Tashauz Oblast. Elected from NTO No. 441, Turkmen SSR. ● Member, Council of

Nationalities Commission on Development of Culture, Language, National and Interethnic Traditions, and Preservation of Historical Heritage.

Shalyev, Atabally Bapbaevich
● Drilling foreman, South Turkmen Exploratory Drilling Administration, "Turkmenburgaz" Trust, "Turkmengazprom" Production Association, Murgabsky Raion, Mary Oblast, Turkmen SSR. CPSU member. Elected from the CPSU. ● Born 1945; Turkmen. Has worked in the petroleum industry since 1963. Member, CPSU CAC since 1986.

From the Ukrainian SSR

Gnatyuk, Viktoriya Vyacheslavovna (F)
● Physician, Central Raion Hospital, Kalinovka, Vinnitsa Oblast. CPSU member. Elected from NTO No. 35, Ukrainian SSR. ● Born 1946; Ukrainian; higher education. Member of USSR SupSov (1984). ● Member, SupSov Committee on Public Health.

Ivashko, Vladimir Antonovich
● First secretary, CC, CP of Ukraine, Kiev. CPSU member. Elected from the CPSU. ● Born 1932; Ukrainian; higher education in mining and economics. Member, CPSU CC since 1989. Bulk of career spent in Party work in Kharkov, later in Dnepropetrovsk. Since 1988, second secretary of Ukrainian CP CC; appointed to current position September 1989 replacing conservative Party leader, Vladimir Shcherbitsky. Has written on the need for socioeconomic reform and struggle against bureaucracy (*Pravda*, July 31, 1989). ● Deputy chairman, CPD Mandate Commission.

Kapto, Aleksandr Semenovich
● Chief, CPSU CC Ideological Department, Moscow. CPSU member. Elected from the All-Union "Znanie" Society. ● Born April 14, 1933; Ukrainian; graduate, Dnepropetrovsk State University; Doctor of Philosophy. Member, CPSU CC since 1986. Extensive experience in Ukrainian Komsomol and CP; worked in 1957–1961 with former KGB chief Viktor Chebrikov in Dnepropetrovsk; "chief ideologist" of Ukrainian Party 1979–1986; Soviet ambassador to Cuba, 1986–1988. Returned to Moscow to CPSU CC *apparat*, 1988. Under his leadership, CC Ideology Department has been involved in elaboration of nationality policy.

Katilevsky, Sergei Mikhailovich
● Leader of a team of blacksmiths, "Voroshilovgradteplovoz" Production Association, Voroshilovgrad. CPSU member. Elected from NTO No. 37, Ukrainian SSR. ● Member, SupSov Committee on Youth.

Kurilenko, Viktor Trifonovich
● Machine operator, "Ukraina" Kolkhoz, Pologovsky Raion, Zaporozhe Oblast. Elected from NTO No. 46, Ukrainian SSR.

Lezhenko, Grigorii Filippovich
● Tunneler, V. I. Lenin Mine, "Krivbassrud" Production Association, Krivoi Rog, Dnepropetrovsk Oblast. CPSU member. Elected from NTO No. 40, Ukrainian SSR. ● Member, SupSov Committee on *Glasnost*, Rights, and Appeals of Citizens.

Oleinik, Boris Ilich
● Poet; secretary, Ukrainian SSR Writers' Union Board, Kiev. CPSU member. Elected from the CPSU. ● Born 1935; Ukrainian. "Establishment reformer," outspoken on ecological problems and republican rights. As leader of the "Greens," helped stop construction of nuclear power plant in Crimea. At CPD, said "the language of the indigenous nation is not a humble timeserver, but the proud master in his own house," but added that the Russian language had "for decades been accepted by the people of our country as a bridge of fraternity" (Central Television, . May 31, 1989). Called for rehabilitation of victims of political oppression of the 1960s and 1970s who, he said, fought for freedoms now commonplace. Seen by Kiev intellectuals as a political weathervane, perhaps with ties to Russian nationalist writers such as Vasilii Belov and Valentin Rasputin. ● Deputy chairman, Council of Nationalities, USSR SupSov; chairman, SupSov Commission to Study the Situation in NKAO.

Romanenko, Viktor Dmitrievich
● Director, Institute of Hydrobiology, Ukrainian SSR Academy of Sciences, Kiev. CPSU member. Elected from the USSR Trade Unions. ● Doctor of Biological Sciences. ● Member, SupSov Committee on Ecology and the Rational Use of Natural Resources.

Shevchenko, Valentina Semenovna (F)
● Chairman, Presidium, Ukrainian SSR SupSov, Kiev. CPSU member. Elected from NTO No. 34, Ukrainian SSR. ● Born 1935; Ukrainian; gradu-

ated Kiev State University; Candidate of Pedagogical Sciences. Member, CPSU CC since 1986. Extensive experience in Ukrainian Komsomol and government organs. 1975–1985, deputy chairman, Presidium, Ukrainian SSR SupSov; named to current post in 1985. Career *apparatchik* who allegedly prevented progressive Ukrainian deputies from addressing the CPD by removing their names from the list of speakers. ● Member, CPD Constitutional Commission; deputy chairman, USSR SupSov Presidium.

Venglovskaya, Vanda Sergeevna (F)
● Weaver, "Sixtieth Anniversary of the Great October Socialist Revolution" Flax Combine, Zhitomir. CPSU member. Elected from NTO No. 44, Ukrainian SSR. ● Was 39 in June 1989. ● Deputy chairman, Council of Nationalities. Member, CPD Drafting Commission; Council of Nationalities Commission on Nationality Policy and Interethnic Relations.

Zabrodin, Ivan Aleksandrovich
● Ukrainian SSR minister of finance, Kiev. CPSU member. Elected from NTO No. 42, Ukrainian SSR. ● Born 1930; Russian; higher education in economics. Worked in financial organs for 40 years. Named to current post in March 1987. ● Member, Council of Nationalities Commission on Consumer Goods, Trade, and Communal and Household Services for the Population.

From the Uzbek SSR

Adylov, Vladimir Tuichievich
● Leader of a team of lathe operators, V. P. Chkalov Aircraft Production Association, Tashkent. CPSU member. Elected from CPSU. ● Member, CPSU CAC since 1986. ● Member, CPD Commission to Investigate Materials Linked with the Activity of the USSR's Prosecutor's Office Investigation Group Headed by Telman Gdlyan; SupSov Committee on Legislation, Legality, and Law and Order; Council of Nationalities Commission on Social and Economic Development of Union and Autonomous Republics, and Autonomous Oblasts and Okrugs.

Atadzhanov, Alikhan Rakhmatovich
● First secretary, Kashka-Darya Obkom. CPSU member. Elected from NTO No. 105, Uzbek SSR. ● Born 1938; Uzbek; graduated from

Tashkent Polytechnical Institute. Until 1988, minister of the gas industry, Uzbek SSR; later deputy chairman, Uzbek SSR Council of Ministers. Appointed to current position, July 1989. Energetic and competent administrator who seems to have kept aloof from Uzbekistan's ongoing cotton scandals. ● Member, Council of Nationalities Commission on Social and Economic Development of Union and Autonomous Republics, and Autonomous Oblasts and Okrugs.

Badalbaeva, Patima (F)
● Chief physician, Shakhrisabz Central Raion Hospital, Kashka-Darya Oblast, Uzbek SSR. CPSU member. Elected from the Soviet Women's Committee. ● Member, SupSov Committee on Women's Affairs, Family Protection, Motherhood, and Childhood.

Davranov, Narzi
● Physician, Sverdlovsk Central Raion Hospital, Zhondor Settlement, Bukhara Oblast. CPSU member. Elected from NTO No. 101, Uzbek SSR. ● Member, SupSov Committee on Public Health.

Efimov, Anatolii Stepanovich
● Chairman, Uzbek SSR People's Control Committee, Tashkent. Elected from NTO No. 109, Uzbek SSR. ● Born 1939; Russian; higher education; experience in Party work (ideology); first secretary, Navoi Obkom, Uzbek SSR until its abolition in 1989. ● Member, SupSov Committee on Defense and State Security.

Khudaibergenova, Rimadzhon Matnazarovna (F)
● First secretary, Khorezm Obkom, Urgench. CPSU member. Elected from NTO No. 127, Uzbek SSR. ● Born late 1930s; Uzbek; graduated from a textile institute and CPSU CC Academy of Social Sciences. Has worked in Party and government in Khorezm since mid-1970s. Appointed to current position in October 1988—the only female obkom first secretary in the USSR. Made her mark as an innovative administrator under Mirkhmat Mirkasymov (now first secretary, Tashkent Obkom) by taking radical steps to solve unemployment and housing problems in Khorezm. Crusader for women's rights in Uzbekistan; her appointment is one of a series in which younger people from nontraditional groups have been promoted to break up old leadership networks—a pattern she herself is now following. ● Member, SupSov Committee on Science, Public Education, Culture, and Upbringing.

Korshunov, Aleksandr Aleksandrovich
● Team leader, V. P. Chkalov Aircraft Production Association, Tashkent. CPSU member. Elected from the USSR Trade Unions. ● For brief statement on making trade unions viable organs for the defense of the interests of working people, see *Pravda*, May 27, 1989. Criticized "extremist" groups—and included among them the Democratic Union and Pamyat—but praised the work of the radical Moscow and Baltic CPD delegations in speech at CPD (Central Television, June 1, 1989). ● Member, CPD Mandate Commission; SupSov Committee on Construction and Architecture.

Nishanov, Rafik Nishanovich
● CPSU member. Elected from NTO No. 123, Uzbek SSR. ● Born January 1926; Uzbek; graduated from Tashkent Pedagogical Institute; Candidate of Historical Sciences. Appointed to current post in June 1989. Held a series of Komsomol and Party posts in Tashkent early in career. 1963, ideology secretary, Uzbek CP CC. Fell out with Uzbek leader Sharif Rashidov in 1970 and was banished to the diplomatic service, serving in Sri Lanka and the Maldive Islands and as Soviet ambassador to Jordan, 1978–1985. Was therefore out of Uzbekistan during the twilight of Rashidov's tenure, when corruption in the republic reached its height. Returned in March 1985 as republican minister of foreign affairs; December 1986, chairman, Uzbek SSR SupSov; January 1988, appointed Uzbek CP CC first secretary. His campaign against corruption climaxed with conviction of Brezhnev's son-in-law in December 1988. Spoke out at CPD against cotton monoculture in Uzbekistan (*Izvestia*, June 2, 1989). Resigned his post in connection with his election to chair the Council of Nationalities. ● Member, CPD Presidium; chairman, USSR SupSov Council of Nationalities; member, USSR SupSov Presidium; first deputy chairman, USSR Parliamentary Group.

Sefershaev, Fikret
● Leader of a cotton-growing team, "Thirtieth Anniversary of the Uzbek SSR" Kolkhoz, Yallama Kishlak, Chinazsky Raion. CPSU member. Elected from NTO No. 121, Uzbek SSR. ● Born 1935; Tatar; has held current position since 1966. Member of USSR SupSov (1984). ● Member, SupSov Committee on Agrarian Questions and Food.

Tso, Vasilii Ivanovich
● General director, Akhunbabaevsky Cotton-Wool Production Associa-

tion, Andizhan. CPSU member. Elected from NTO No. 98, Uzbek SSR. ● Member, Council of Nationalities Commission on Consumer Goods, Trade, and Communal and Household Services for the Population.

Zokirov, Munavarkhon Zakriyaevich
● Chief, DOSAAF Sports and Technical Club, Kasansai Raion, Namangan Oblast, Uzbek SSR. Elected from the USSR DOSAAF. ● Member, SupSov Committee on Defense and State Security.

From the Abkhaz ASSR (Georgian SSR)

Ardzinba, Vladislav Grigorevich
● Director, D. I. Gulia Abkhaz Institute of Language, Literature, and History, Georgian SSR Academy of Sciences, Sukhumi Raion. CPSU member. Elected from NTO No. 486, Abkhaz ASSR. ● Abkhaz; Doctor of Historical Sciences. Complained at CPD about discrimination against the Abkhaz and called for them to have their own Union republic (Central Television, June 2, 1989). ● Member, Council of Nationalities Commission on Nationality Policy and Interethnic Relations.

Arshba, Ruslan Ardevanovich
● Shaft-sinker, Mine No. 2, "Tkvarchelskoe" Mining Administration, Tkvarcheli. CPSU member. Elected from NTO No. 491, Abkhaz ASSR. ● Born 1952; Abkhaz. Member of USSR SupSov (1984). ● Member, Council of Nationalities Commission on Social and Economic Development of Union and Autonomous Republics, and Autonomous Oblasts and Okrugs.

Cholokyan, Karzui Sarkisovna (F)
● Kolkhoz member, Rustavli Kolkhoz, Gulripshsky Raion. CPSU member. Elected from NTO No. 488, Abkhaz ASSR. ● Member, SupSov Committee on Ecology and the Rational Use of Natural Resources.

Salukvadze, Revaz Georgievich
● Director, I. N. Vekua Physico-Technical Institute, Sukhumi. CPSU member. Elected from NTO No. 481, Abkhaz SSR. ● Member, SupSov Committee on Economic Reform.

From the Adzhar ASSR (Georgian SSR)

Badzhelidze, Nino Usupovna (F)
● Tea grower at Khutsubani Village Kolkhoz, Kobuletsky Raion. Elected from NTO No. 501, Adzhar ASSR. ● Member, SupSov Committee on Women's Affairs, Family Protection, Motherhood, and Childhood.

Buachidze, Tengiz Pavlovich
● Chairman, Georgian Cultural Foundation, Tbilisi. CPSU member. Elected from NTO No. 493, Adzhar ASSR. ● Born November 7, 1926. Doctor of Philological Sciences. Prolific writer on contemporary Georgian literature and its relations with those of other republics. Member, CC, CP of Georgia. ● Member, CPD Constitutional Oversight Commission.

Gogeshvili, Aleko Rafaelovich
● Assembler, Batumi Transformer Plant. CPSU member. Elected from NTO No. 495, Adzhar ASSR. ● Member, SupSov Committee on Veterans and Invalids.

Sakandelidze, Iamze Binalovna (F)
● Tobacco grower, Merisi Kolkhoz, Kedsky Raion. Elected from NTO No. 497, Adzhar ASSR.

From the Bashkir ASSR (RSFSR)

Nikolaev, Vasilii Vasilevich
● Administrator, "Kaustik" Production Association, Sterlitamak. Elected from NTO No. 509, Bashkir ASSR. ● Member, SupSov Committee on Ecology and the Rational Use of Natural Resources.

Prokushev, Vladimir Ivanovich
● *Pravda* correspondent for the Bashkir ASSR, Ufa. CPSU member. Elected from NTO No. 505, Bashkir ASSR. ● Member, SupSov Committee on Soviets of Peoples' Deputies, Development of Government, and Self-Government.

Safin, Minikhalaf Mustafaivich
● Chairman, Lenin Kolkhoz, Neftekamsk, Krasnokamsky Raion. CPSU member. Elected from NTO No. 510, Bashkir ASSR. ● Member, Council of Nationalities Commission on Development of Culture, Language, National and Interethnic Traditions, and Preservation of Historical Heritage.

Sharipov, Yurii Kamalovich
● General director, S. M. Kirov Production Association, Ufa. CPSU member. Elected from NTO No. 506, Bashkir ASSR. ● CPD speech called for every Soviet family to be provided with a telephone. Revealed statistics about the lack of access to telephones in the USSR, especially in rural areas (*Izvestia*, June 26, 1989). ● Member, SupSov Committee on Defense and State Security.

From the Buryat ASSR (RSFSR)

Angapov, Semen Vasilevich
● Pensioner, Ulan-Ude, Buryat ASSR. CPSU member. Elected from the All-Union Organization of War and Labor Veterans. ● Until retirement was deputy chairman, Buryat ASSR Council of Ministers. ● Member, Council of Nationalities Commission on Nationality Policy and Interethnic Relations.

Kalashnikov, Vladimir Yakovlevich
● Director, "Erdem" Sovkhoz, Mukhorshibirsky Raion. CPSU member. Elected from NTO No. 519, Buryat ASSR. ● Member, SupSov Committee on Women's Affairs, Family Protection, Motherhood, and Childhood.

Litvintseva, Galina Nikolaevna (F)
● Leader of a team of interior decorators, "Zhilgrazhdanstroi" Trust's No. 7 Construction and Installation Administration, Ulan-Ude. CPSU member. Elected from NTO No. 516, Buryat ASSR. ● Member, SupSov Committee on Construction and Architecture.

Stepanova, Galina Sambuevna (F)
● Organizer, Extracurricular and Extramural Education Work, Onokhoi Secondary School, Zaigraevsky Raion. CPSU member. Elected from NTO

No. 521, Buryat ASSR. ● Member, Council of Nationalities Commission on Development of Culture, Language, National and Interethnic Traditions, and Preservation of Historical Heritage.

From the Chechen-Ingush ASSR (RSFSR)

Darsigov, Musa Yusupovich
● Team leader, "Alkhanchurtsky" Sovkhoz, Malgobeksky Raion. CPSU member. Elected from NTO No. 674, Chechen-Ingush ASSR. ● At session of SupSov Council of Nationalities called for the creation of an Ingush ASSR within the RSFSR (Ingush autonomy was abolished by Stalin in 1934) (Central Television, June 6, 1989). ● Member, Council of Nationalities Commission on Nationality Policy and Interethnic Relations.

Foteev, Vladimir Konstantinovich
● CPSU member. Elected from NTO No. 675, Chechen-Ingush ASSR. ● Born June 25, 1935; Russian; graduate of Moscow Aviation Technology Institute and Higher Party School. Member, CPSU CC since 1986. 1976–1983, worked in CPSU CC *apparat*; 1984, appointed first secretary, Chechen-Ingush Obkom; June 1989, resigned that post when appointed to chair SupSov committee. Attacked by *Pravda* in 1987 for taking punitive action against author of a critical letter. Has spoken out against the MDG, on grounds it would have negative effect on unity of SupSov (TASS, July 31, 1989). ● Member, USSR SupSov Presidium; chairman, USSR SupSov Committee on *Glasnost*, Rights, and Appeals of Citizens.

Nemtsev, Evgenii Ivanovich
● Leader of a repair team, "Elektropribor" Plant, "Orgtekhnika" Production Association, Groznyi. CPSU member. Elected from NTO No. 671, Chechen-Ingush ASSR. ● Member, SupSov Committee on Defense and State Security.

Umalatova, Sazhi Zaindinovna (F)
● Leader of a multiskilled team, "Krasnyi Molot" Machine Building Plant, Groznyi. CPSU member. Elected from the CPSU. ● Born 1953; Chechen. Has worked at current enterprise since 1969. Member of USSR SupSov (1984). ● Member, SupSov Committee on Soviets of People's Deputies, Development of Government, and Self-Government.

From the Chuvash ASSR (RSFSR)

Dmitriev, Aleksei Aleksandrovich
● Machine operator, "Slava" Kolkhoz, Lash-Tayaba, Yalchiksky Raion. CPSU member. Elected from NTO No. 683, Chuvash ASSR.

Fedorov, Nikolai Vasilevich
● Senior Lecturer, Chuvash State University, Cheboksary. CPSU member. Elected from NTO No. 681, Chuvash ASSR. ● Member, SupSov Committee on Legislation, Legality, and Law and Order.

Mikhailova, Lidiya Ivanovna (F)
● Teacher, secondary school, Shorshely, Mariinsko-Posadsky Raion. CPSU member. Elected from NTO No. 685, Chuvash ASSR. ● Member, SupSov Committee on Science, Public Education, Culture, and Upbringing.

Valentinov, Leonid Fedorovich
● Road-grader operator with the "Spetsstroimekhanizatsiya" Trust, Cheboksary. CPSU member. Elected from NTO No. 680, Chuvash ASSR. ● Member, SupSov Committee on Ecology and the Rational Use of Natural Resources.

From the Dagestan ASSR (RSFSR)

Gorbachev, Aleksandr Grigorevich
● Director, "Rossiya" Sovkhoz, Kizlyarsky Raion. CPSU member. Elected from NTO No. 531, Dagestan ASSR. ● Member, Council of Nationalities Commission on Social and Economic Development of Union and Autonomous Republics, and Autonomous Oblasts and Okrugs.

Kakhirov, Kurbanmagomed Zulfikarovich
● Team leader, "Leninsky" Sovkhoz, Magaramkentsky Raion. CPSU member. Elected from NTO No. 533, Dagestan ASSR. ● Member, SupSov Committee on Agrarian Questions and Food.

Magomedov, Gadzhimurad Mamedovich
● First secretary, Sergokalinsky Raikom. CPSU member. Elected from NTO No. 529, Dagestan ASSR. ● Member, Council of Nationalities Commission on Consumer Goods, Trade, and Communal and Household Services for the Population.

Zainalkhanov, Dalgat Gadzhievich
● Docker and machine operator, maritime commercial port, Makhachkala. Elected from NTO No. 526, Dagestan ASSR. ● Member, Council of Nationalities Commission on Development of Culture, Language, National and Interethnic Traditions, and Preservation of Historical Heritage.

From the Kabardino-Balkar ASSR (RSFSR)

Karpenko, Valentin Filippovich
● Leader of a team of metalworkers, remote-control equipment plant, Nalchik. CPSU member. Elected from NTO No. 538, Kabardino-Balkar ASSR. ● Member, Council of Nationalities Commission on Consumer Goods, Trade, and Communal and Household Goods for the Population.

Kuliev, Sultan Oyusovich
● Livestock unit chief, Lenin Kolkhoz, Chegemsky Raion. CPSU member. Elected from NTO No. 545, Kabardino-Balkar ASSR.

Umerenkov, Aleksei Mikhailovich
● Chairman, "Zhuk" Kolkhoz, Prokhladnensky Raion. CPSU member. Elected from NTO No. 542, Kabardino-Balkar ASSR. ● Member, SupSov Committee on Agrarian Questions and Food.

Zhigunova, Lyudmila Tazretovna (F)
● Chief, Children's Department, First-Aid Clinical Hospital, Nalchik. Elected from NTO No. 536, Kabardino-Balkar ASSR. ● Member, SupSov Committee on Public Health.

From the Kalmyk ASSR (RSFSR)

Buraev, Ivan Zambaevich
● Head of the "Fortieth Anniversary of October" Kolkhoz machine workshops, Sarpinsky Raion. Elected from NTO No. 554, Kalmyk ASSR.

Kugultinov, David Nikitich
● Writer; chairman, Kalmyk ASSR Writers' Union Board. CPSU member. Elected from NTO No. 550, Kalmyk ASSR. ● Kalmyk. Called for a law defending the rights of AIDS victims, especially mothers and children, noting that the United States had adopted a law penalizing those guilty of discrimination against AIDS victims (*Izvestia*, February 23, 1989). Proposed restoration of Crimean and German autonomy (Central Television, June 6, 1989). ● Member, Council of Nationalities Commission on Development of Culture, Language, National and Interethnic Traditions, and Preservation of Historical Heritage.

Nikitin, Vladilen Valentinovich
● First deputy chairman, RSFSR State Agroindustrial Committee (Gosagroprom), RSFSR minister of agriculture. CPSU member. Elected from NTO No. 553, Kalmyk ASSR. ● Born 1936; Russian; graduated from Omsk Agricultural Institute and Higher Party School. 1976–1985, chairman, Tyumen Oblispolkom. Member of USSR SupSov (1984). Candidate member, CPSU CC since 1986. ● Member, SupSov Committee on Agrarian Questions and Food.

Ochirov, Valerii Nikolaevich
● Colonel; air force regiment commander. CPSU member. Elected from NTO No. 548, Kalmyk ASSR. ● Born 1951; Kalmyk; graduated from higher aviation college and military-political academy. Veteran of Afghan war. Hero of the Soviet Union. ● Member, SupSov Committee on Defense and State Security.

From the Karakalpak ASSR (Uzbek SSR)

Abdimuratova, Shukir (F)
● Family contract worker, "Pravda" State Farm, Shumanai Raion. Elected from NTO No. 567, Karakalpak ASSR. ● Member, SupSov Committee on Legislation, Legality and Law and Order.

Ibragimov, Mirzaolim Ibragimovich
● Chairman, Presidium, Uzbek SSR SupSov, Tashkent. CPSU member. Elected from NTO No. 562, Karakalpak ASSR. ● Was 61 in March 1989. Educator. Former leader of Uzbek Komsomol, the republic's minister of the cotton cleaning industry, and chairman of its Committee for Physical Culture and Sports. Was Uzbekistan's representative at USSR Council of Ministers until election to current job in March 1989. ● Member, CPD Drafting Commission; deputy chairman, USSR SupSov Presidium.

Kaipbergenov, Tulepbergen
● Writer; chairman, Karakalpak ASSR Writers' Union Board. CPSU member. Elected from NTO No. 566, Karakalpak ASSR. ● Spoke at CPD on the disastrous ecological situation of the Aral Sea: "People in the area die unnatural deaths. . . . Is there any other state in the world where the poisoning of its own population is permitted?" (Central Television, May 30, 1989). Called for cut in cotton production and designation of Aral Sea area as ecological disaster zone. ● Member, CPD Drafting Commission;member, Council of Nationalities Commission on Development of Culture, Language, National and Interethnic Traditions, and Preservation of Historical Heritage.

Pershin, Andrei Leonidovich
● Excavator operator, Production Repair and Operation Association, Kungrad Raion. Elected from NTO No. 561, Karakalpak ASSR. ● Member, SupSov Committee on Economic Reform.

From the Karelian ASSR (RSFSR)

Afanaseva, Lyudmila Vladimirovna (F)
● Chief physician, No. 1 Maternity Home, Petrozavodsk. Elected from NTO No. 569, Karelian ASSR. ● Member, SupSov Committee on Women's Affairs, Family Protection, Motherhood, and Childhood.

Demidov, Mikhail Vasilevich
● First secretary, Kalevala Raikom. CPSU member. Elected from NTO No. 573, Karelian ASSR. ● Member, Council of Nationalities Commission on Social and Economic Development of Union and Autonomous Republics, and Autonomous Oblasts and Okrugs.

Genchev, Anatolii Aleksandrovich
● Senior engineer and flight safety inspector, Petrozavodsk Aircraft Enterprise. CPSU member. Elected from NTO No. 571, Karelian ASSR.
● Member, Council of Nationalities Commission on Nationality Policy and Interethnic Relations.

Pilnikov, Stanislav Vasilevich
● Teacher, No. 1 secondary school, Pitkyaranta. CPSU member. Elected from NTO No. 576, Karelian ASSR. ● Member, SupSov Committee on Youth.

From the Komi ASSR (RSFSR)

Chernykh, Galina Aleksandrovna (F)
● Director, Secondary School, Obyachevo, Priluzsky Raion. CPSU member. Elected from NTO No. 588, Komi ASSR. ● Member, Council of Nationalities Commission on Development of Culture, Language, and National and Interethnic Traditions, and Preservation of Historical Heritage.

Ignatov, Stepan Vladimirovich
● Chief economist, "Pomozdinsky" Sovkhoz, Ust-Kulomsky Raion. CPSU member. Elected from NTO No. 590, Komi ASSR. ● Member, Council of Nationalities Commission on Social and Economic Development of Union and Autonomous Republics, and Autonomous Oblasts and Okrugs.

Lushchikov, Sergei Gennadevich
● Deputy Minister of Justice, Komi ASSR. CPSU member. Elected from NTO No. 580, Komi ASSR. ● Member, SupSov Committee on Legislation, Legality, and Law and Order.

Maksimov, Valerii Nikolaevich
● Team leader, "Severnaya" Coal Mine, "Vorkutaugol" Production Association, Vorkuta. Elected from NTO No. 583, Komi ASSR.
● Member, SupSov Committee on Ecology and the Rational Use of Natural Resources.

From the Mari ASSR (RSFSR)

Karpochev, Vladimir Andreevich
● Chairman, "Put Lenina" Kolkhoz, Volzhsky Raion. CPSU member. Elected from NTO No. 597, Mari ASSR. ● Member, SupSov Committee on Agrarian Questions and Food.

Nikitin, Rudolf Ivanovich
● General director, "Izotop" Production Association, Yoshkar-Ola. CPSU member. Elected from NTO No. 593, Mari ASSR. ● Member, SupSov Committee on Defense and State Security.

Samsonov, Nikolai Alekseevich
● Lathe operator, Fiftieth Anniversary of the USSR "Kontakt" Plant, Yoshkar-Ola. Elected from NTO No. 592, Mari ASSR. ● Member, SupSov Committee on Economic Reform.

Vedenkina, Zinaida Alekseevna (F)
● Trolleybus driver, Trolleybus Transport Directorate, Yoshkar-Ola, Mari ASSR. Elected from the USSR Trade Unions. ● Member, Council of Nationalities Commission on Consumer Goods, Trade, and Communal and Household Services for the Population.

From the Mordovian ASSR (RSFSR)

Aliluev, Nikolai Ivanovich
● Machine operator, Ruzaevka Station Locomotive Depot, Kuibyshev Railroad. CPSU member. Elected from NTO No. 610, Mordovian ASSR. ● Member, Council of Nationalities Commission on Social and Economic Development of Union and Autonomous Republics, and Autonomous Oblasts and Okrugs.

Kulikov, Evgenii Andreevich
● Chairman, Lenin Kolkhoz, Dubensky Raion. CPSU member. Elected from NTO No. 606, Mordovian ASSR. ● Born 1927; Mordovian. Member of USSR SupSov (1984).

Levakin, Vyacheslav Alekseevich
● Director general, "Svetotekhnika" Production Association, Saransk. CPSU member. Elected from NTO No. 604, Mordovian ASSR. ● Member, Council of Nationalities Commission on Consumer Goods, Trade, and Communal and Household Services for the Population.

Maslakova, Anna Polikarpovna (F)
● Team leader, "Rezinotekhnika" Plant, Saransk. CPSU member. Elected from NTO No. 603, Mordovian ASSR. ● Member, SupSov Committee on Veterans and Invalids.

From the Nakhichevan ASSR (Azerbaijan SSR)

Abasov, Kurban Abas Kuli ogly
● General director, "Kaspmorneftegaz" Production Association, Baku. CPSU member. Elected from NTO No. 619, Nakhichevan ASSR. ● Born 1926; Azerbaijani; higher education. Member of USSR SupSov (1984). Campaign platform for CPD elections focused on local issues (*Izvestia*, March 30, 1989). ● Member, SupSov Committee on Construction and Architecture.

Isaev, Geidar Isa ogly
● First secretary, Nakhichevan Obkom, Azerbaijan SSR. CPSU member. Elected from NTO No. 615, Nakhichevan ASSR. ● Born 1936; Azerbaijani; Candidate of Geological Sciences. Former chairman, Council of Ministers, Nakhichevan ASSR. ● Member, Council of Nationalities Commission on Social and Economic Development of Union and Autonomous Republics, and Autonomous Oblasts and Okrugs.

Kerimov, Dzhangir Ali Abbas ogly
● Department head, Academy of Social Sciences of CPSU CC, Moscow. CPSU member. Elected from NTO No. 623, Nakhichevan ASSR. ● Born 1923; Doctor of Jurisprudence; professor. Corresponding member, USSR Academy of Sciences. Author of several works on government and law. ● Member, CPD Constitutional Commission; Constitutional Oversight Commission; SupSov Committee on Legislation, Legality, and Law and Order.

Nagiev, Ramazan Shamy ogly
● Engineer, Dzhulfa Locomotive Depot, Azerbaijan Railroad. CPSU member. Elected from NTO No. 617, Nakhichevan ASSR.

From the North Ossetian ASSR (RSFSR)

Aguzarova, Stella Borisovna (F)
● Metalworker, "Fiftieth Anniversary of the Komsomol" Electric Light Plant, Ordzhonikidze. CPSU member. Elected from NTO No. 627, North Ossetian ASSR. ● Member, Council of Nationalities Commission on Social and Economic Development of Union and Autonomous Republics, and Autonomous Oblasts and Okrugs.

Byazyrova, Valentina Timofeevna (F)
● Teacher, Secondary School No. 5, Ordzhonikidze. CPSU member. Elected from NTO No. 624, North Ossetian ASSR. ● Member, SupSov Committee on Science, Public Education, Culture, and Upbringing.

Ikaev, Georgii Dzambulatovich
● First secretary, Digora Raikom. CPSU member. Elected from NTO No. 630, North Ossetian ASSR. ● Member, Council of Nationalities Commission on Nationality Policy and Interethnic Relations.

Nyrkov, Anatolii Ivanovich
● Machine setter, Ordzhonikidze Glass Plant. Elected from NTO No. 625, North Ossetian ASSR. ● Member, SupSov Committee on *Glasnost*, Rights, and Appeals of Citizens.

From the Tatar ASSR (RSFSR)

Buravov, Gennadii Vladimirovich
● Diesel locomotive engineer, Bugulma Locomotive Depot of the Kuibyshev Railroad. Elected from NTO No. 638, Tatar ASSR.

Kamenshchikova, Galina Nikolaevna (F)
● Chief physician, children's department, Central Raion Hospital,

Zelenodolsk. CPSU member. Elected from NTO No. 640, Tatar ASSR.
● Member, SupSov Committee on Public Health.

Minnullin, Tufan Abdullovich
● Writer, Kazan. CPSU member. Elected from NTO No. 643, Tatar ASSR.
● Born August 25, 1935; Tatar; higher education; dramatist and fiction
writer who was chairman, Tatar ASSR Writers' Union Board until May
1989. See *Literaturnaya Rossiya*, No. 17, 1989, for sympathetic comments on Tatar nationalist groups "struggling for the preservation of
their native culture." Spoke at CPD on ecological and nationality issues;
complained about the construction of a nuclear power station on the
Kama River and about the unequal representation of the ASSRs in the
CPD and SupSov as compared to that of the Union Republics. Also
complained about discrimination against Tatars and other nationalities
(Central Television, June 6, 1989). Stressed the importance of national
culture in resolving economic and social problems (interview with Radio
Moscow, July 4, 1989). ● Member, Council of Nationalities Commission
on Development of Culture, Language, National and Interethnic Traditions, and Preservation of Historical Heritage.

Mukhametzyanov, Mukharam Timergalievich
● Chairman, "Iskra" Kolkhoz, Buinsky Raion, Tatar ASSR. CPSU
member. Elected from the Council of Kolkhozes. ● Tatar. Called upon
CPD for efforts to resolve interethnic problems, expressing concern that
some nationalities are "more equal than others" (*Sovetskaya Rossiya*,
June 14, 1989). ● Member, Council of Nationalities Commission on
Social and Economic Development of Union and Autonomous Repub-
lics, and Autonomous Oblasts and Okrugs.

From the Tuva ASSR (RSFSR)

Kara-Sal, Damdyn Bazyievich
● Director, "Tuvinsky" Sovkhoz, Teve-Khaya, Dzun-Khemchiksky Raion.
CPSU member. Elected from NTO No. 650, Tuva ASSR. ● Member,
SupSov Committee on Soviets of People's Deputies, Development of
Government, and Self-Government.

Komarov, Yurii Trofimovich
● General director, V. I. Lenin "Tuvaasbest" Combine, Ak-Dovurak.
CPSU member. Elected from NTO No. 649, Tuva ASSR. ● Member,
SupSov Committee on Construction and Architecture.

Lapygin, Vladimir Lavrentevich
● General designer and director, Automation and Instrument Making
Scientific Production Association, Moscow. CPSU member. Elected from
NTO No. 656, Tuva ASSR. ● Born 1925; Russian. Graduated Moscow
Aviation Institute (1952); Doctor of Technical Sciences. Hero of Socialist
Labor. Specialist in missile guidance systems; leading figure in the Soviet
military-industrial complex; previously director of the "Kosmonavtika"
Scientific Production Association, a principal contractor on the Soviet
space shuttle project. Member of USSR SupSov (1984). Lapygin has
advocated the creation of a professional Soviet army, arguing that
military technology is developing so fast that conscripts are not able to
deal with it. Moderately conservative. Heads SupSov committee overseeing defense and security organs; said at his confirmation hearings
that, although monitoring of KGB activity was necessary, indiscriminate
criticism was not (TASS, June 26, 1989). ● Member, USSR SupSov
Presidium; chairman, SupSov Committee on Defense and State Security.

Sanchat, Aleksandr Sandanovich
● First secretary, Tes-Khemsky Komsomol Raikom. CPSU member.
Elected from NTO No. 655, Tuva ASSR. ● Member, SupSov Committee
on Youth.

From the Udmurt ASSR (RSFSR)

Danilov, Sergei Nikolaevich
● Livestock farmer and leaseholder, "Shafeevsky" Sovkhoz, Yukamensky
Raion. CPSU member. Elected from NTO No. 663, Udmurt ASSR.
● Member, SupSov Committee on *Glasnost*, Rights, and Appeals of
Citizens.

Engver, Nikolai Nikolaevich
● Chief scientific associate, Physical-Technical Institute, Urals Department, USSR Academy of Sciences, Izhevsk. CPSU member. Elected from

NTO No. 658, Udmurt ASSR. ● Born in a Stalinist prison camp. Aged 50 in 1989. Educated as an economist at Moscow State University. Emerged as a progressive leader in the SupSov. Election platform proposed strict SupSov control over budget and ministerial appointments, so that ministers would have to account for all the money the SupSov appropriated to them (Central Television, June 7, 1989). Called the July 1989 miners' strikes a "gigantic step forward." (*Baltimore Sun*, August 6, 1989). For detailed portrait, see *New York Times Magazine*, August 27, 1989.
● Member, CPD Drafting Commission; SupSov Committee on Youth.

Korobkin, Vladimir Vladimirovich
● Chief, Norms and Standards Department, "Izhevsky Motozavod" Production Association, Izhevsk. CPSU member. Elected from NTO No. 659, Udmurt ASSR. ● Member, Council of Nationalities Commission on Consumer Goods, Trade, and Communal and Household Services for the Population.

Murashov, Vladimir Konstantinovich
● Team leader, Lenin Kolkhoz, Seltinsky Raion. CPSU member. Elected from NTO No. 667, Udmurt ASSR.

From the Yakut ASSR (RSFSR)

Boikov, Sergei Vladimirovich
● Leader of a team of metalworkers, Mechanized Column No. 154, "Bamstroimekhanizatsiya" Trust, Aldan. Elected from NTO No. 693, Yakut ASSR. ● Proposed Eltsin's candidacy for chairman of the USSR People's Control Committee (Central Television, June 7, 1989).
● Member, Council of Nationalities Commission on Social and Economic Development of Union and Autonomous Republics, and Autonomous Oblasts and Okrugs.

Larionov, Vladimir Petrovich
● Deputy chairman, Presidium, Yakutsk Scientific Center, Siberian Department, USSR Academy of Sciences; director, Institute of Physical and Technical Problems of the Arctic. CPSU member. Elected from the CPSU. ● Born 1938. ● Member, SupSov Committee on Science, Public Education, Culture, and Upbringing.

Mikheev, Mikhail Alekseevich
● Leader of multiskilled team, "Uglestroi-1" Construction Administration, "Yakutuglestroi" Combine, Neryungri. CPSU member. Elected from NTO No. 699, Yakut ASSR. ● Member, SupSov Committee on Construction and Architecture.

Osipov, Prokopii Dmitrievich
● Secretary, Party Committee for Enterprises and Organizations, Vilyusk Hydroelectric Power Station, Chernyshevsky Settlement, Mirninsky Raion. CPSU member. Elected from NTO No. 696, Yakut ASSR. ● Member, SupSov Committee on Ecology and the Rational Use of Natural Resources.

From the Adygei Autonomous Oblast (RSFSR)

Dmitriev, Vladimir Vasilevich
● Worker, Pervomaisky Timber Processing Establishment, Maikop Raion. CPSU member. Elected from NTO No. 702, Adygei Autonomous Oblast. ● Member, SupSov Committee on Youth.

Mashbashev, Iskhak Shumafovich
● Writer; responsible secretary, Adygei Writers' Organization, Maikop. CPSU member. Elected from NTO No. 705, Adygei Autonomous Oblast. ● Member, Council of Nationalities Commission on Nationality Policy and Interethnic Relations.

From the Gorno-Altai Autonomous Oblast (RSFSR)

Erelina, Valentina Kuzukovna (F)
● Director, Sugash Secondary School, Ust-Koksinsky Raion. Elected from NTO No. 709, Gorno-Altai Autonomous Oblast. ● Member, Council of Nationalities Commission on Development of Culture, Language, National and Interethnic Traditions, and Preservation of Historical Heritage.

Mironova, Dagmara Sergeevna (F)
● Weaver, cotton textile combine, Barnaul, Altai Krai. CPSU member. Elected from the USSR Trade Unions. ● Member, SupSov Committee on Public Health.

From the Gorno-Badakhshan Autonomous Oblast (RSFSR)

Khudonazarov, Davlatnazar
● First secretary, Tajik SSR Cinematographers' Union Board, Dushanbe. CPSU member. Elected from NTO No. 711, Gorno-Badakhshan Autonomous Oblast. ● Member, SupSov Committee on Science, Public Education, Culture, and Upbringing.

Navruzov, Sherkhonbek
● Team leader, "Vakhon" Sovkhoz, Ishkashimsky Raion. CPSU member. Elected from NTO No. 713, Gorno-Badakhshan Autonomous Oblast.
● Member, Council of Nationalities Commission on Social and Economic Development of Union and Autonomous Republics, and Autonomous Oblasts and Okrugs.

From the Jewish Autonomous Oblast (RSFSR)

Danilyuk, Nikolai Nikolaevich
● Chairman, Khabarovsk Kraiispolkom, RSFSR. CPSU member. Elected from NTO No. 720, Jewish Autonomous Oblast. ● Member of delegation that met with Japanese offficials in September 1987 in Khabarovsk to discuss Soviet control of the Kurile Islands. ● Member, SupSov Committee on Soviets of People's Deputies, Development of Government, and Self-Government.

Khitron, Pavel Abramovich
● Director, "Amursky" Sovkhoz, Oktyabrsky Raion. CPSU member. Elected from NTO No. 717, Jewish Autonomous Oblast. ● Member, SupSov Committee on *Glasnost*, Rights, and Appeals of Citizens.

From the Karachaevo-Cherkess Autonomous Oblast (RSFSR)

Kangliev, Andrei Yakhyaevich
● Truck driver, "Erken-Shakharsky" Fruit Sovkhoz, Adygei-Khablsky Raion. CPSU member. Elected from NTO No. 722, Karachaevo-Cherkess Autonomous Oblast. ● Member, Council of Nationalities Commission on Social and Economic Development of Union and Autonomous Republics, and Autonomous Oblasts and Okrugs.

Petrova, Lyudmila Nikolaevna (F)
● General director, "Niva Stavropolya" Scientific Production Association, Stavropol, RSFSR. CPSU member. Elected from VASKhNIL. ● Expressed concern that changes are taking place too quickly (*Izvestia*, May 24, 1989). ● Member, SupSov Committee on Economic Reform.

From the Khakass Autonomous Oblast (RSFSR)

Batynskaya, Lyudmila Ivanovna (F)
● Correspondent for Krasnodar Krai and Tuva ASSR, *Izvestia*; editor, *Krasnoyarsky komsomolets*, Krasnoyarsk, RSFSR. CPSU member. Elected from the USSR Journalists' Union. ● Born 1950; higher education. For electoral statement on need for professionalism among journalists and her intention to work for a broader network of youth publications, see *Pravda*, February 2, 1989. ● Member, Council of Nationalities Commission on Development of Culture, Language, National and Interethnic Traditions, and Preservation of Historical Heritage.

Botandaev, Iosif Nikiforovich
● Driver, "Tuimsky" Sovkhoz, Shirinsky Raion. CPSU member. Elected from NTO No. 735, Khakass Autonomous Oblast.

From the Nagorno-Karabakh Autonomous Oblast (Azerbaijan SSR)

Dzhafarov, Vagif Dzhafar ogly
- First secretary, Shusha Raikom. CPSU member. Elected from NTO No. 730, Nagorno-Karabakh Autonomous Oblast. ● Azerbaijani. Disputed Armenian claim that deputies from the Nagorno-Karabakh Autonomoius Oblast had been unfairly elected to the Council of People's Deputies (Central Television, May 30, 1989). ● Member, SupSov Committee on *Glasnost*, Rights, and Appeals of Citizens.

Pogosyan, Genrikh Andreevich
- Pensioner. CPSU member. Elected from NTO No. 726, Nagorno-Karabakh Autonomous Oblast. ● Born 1931; Armenian; higher agricultural education. Former Party first secretary, NKAO; retired January 1989 after being criticized for allegedly nationalist policies (*Izvestia*, January 19, 1989). In 1988, Pogosyan strongly supported demands for the transfer of Nagorno-Karabakh to Armenia; called for a change in the Soviet Constitution and for Nagorno-Karabakh to be granted autonomous republic status (APN, August 25, 1988). ● Member, Council of Nationalities Commission on Nationality Policy and Interethnic Relations.

From the South Ossetian Autonomous Oblast (Georgian SSR)

Khugaeva, Diana Varlamovna (F)
- Leader, lease collective, Chasavalsky Stock Unit, Kirovsky Sovkhoz, Dzhavsky Raion. Elected from NTO No. 739, South Ossetian Autonomous Oblast. ● Member, SupSov Committee on Youth.

Tedeev, Lev Radzhenovich
- Machine operator, Znaursky Raion Machinery and Tractor Pool Repairs and Operations Enterprise, Dzagina, Znaursky Raion, South Ossetian Autonomous Oblast. Elected NTO No. 739, South Ossetian Autonomous Oblast.

From the Agin-Buryat Autonomous Okrug (RSFSR)

Nimbuev, Tsyren
● General chairman, "Mogoituiskoe" Agroindustrial Association, Mogoitui Settlement. CPSU member. Elected from NTO No. 741, Agin-Buryat Autonomous Okrug. ● Member, SupSov Committee on Legislation, Legality, and Law and Order.

From the Chukot Autonomous Okrug (RSFSR)

Etylen, Vladimir Mikhailovich
● Postgraduate student, Academy of Social Sciences of CPSU CC. CPSU member. Elected from NTO No. 748, Chukot Autonomous Okrug, Magadan Oblast, RSFSR. ● Member, SupSov Committee on International Affairs.

From the Evenki Autonomous Okrug (RSFSR)

Mongo, Mikhail Innokentevich
● Chief, Department for Affairs of Northern and Arctic Ethnic Groups, Krasnoyarsk Kraiispolkom. CPSU member. Elected from NTO No. 749, Evenki Autonomous Okrug. ● Spoke at CPD on behalf of the northern peoples of the USSR, saying the average life expectancy of the ethnic groups in the USSR's northern regions was 16–18 years below the country as a whole (*Pravda*, June 7, 1989). ● Member, Council of Nationalities Commission on Nationality Policy and Interethnic Relations.

From the Khanti-Mansi Autonomous Okrug (RSFSR)

Aipin, Eremei Danilovich
● Writer; senior editor at the House of Creativity of the Northern Ethnic

Groups, Tyumen Oblast. CPSU member. Elected from NTO No. 747, Khanty-Mansi Autonomous Okrug. ● Born 1948; Khant. Electoral platform dedicated to preventing the extinction of the Khant nation (*Moskovskie novosti*, January 8 and March 19, 1989). ● Member, Council of Nationalities Commission on Nationality Policy and Interethnic Relations.

From the Komi-Permyak Autonomous Okrug (RSFSR)

Khomyakov, Aleksandr Ivanovich
● Chairman, "Rodina" Kolkhoz, Kochevsky Raion. CPSU member. Elected from NTO No. 742, Komi-Permyak Autonomous Okrug. ● Member, Council of Nationalities Commission on Consumer Goods, Trade, and Communal and Household Services for the Population.

From the Koryak Autonomous Okrug (RSFSR)

Kosygin, Vladimir Vladimirovich
● Correspondent, Television and Radio Broadcasting Committee, Kamchatka Oblast. CPSU member. Elected from NTO No. 743, Koryak Autonomous Okrug. ● Born 1933; higher education. Prolific author. ● Member, CPD Constitutional Commission; member, Council of Nationalities Commission on Union and Autonomous Republics, and Autonomous Oblasts and Okrugs.

From the Nenets Autonomous Okrug (RSFSR)

Vyucheisky, Aleksandr Ivanovich
● Chief, Rolling and Repair Shop, Khoreiver Oil and Gas Prospecting Expedition, Naryan Mar, Arkhangelsk Oblast. CPSU member. Elected from NTO No. 744, Nenetsk Autonomous Okrug. ● Member, Council of Nationalities Commission on Social and Economic Development of Union and Autonomous Republics, and Autonomous Republics and Okrugs.

From the Taimyr (Dolgano-Nenets) Autonomous Okrug (RSFSR)

Palchin, Semen Yakovlevich
● Director, "Tukhard" Sovkhoz, Ust-Eniseisky Raion. Elected from NTO No. 745, Taimyr Autonomous Okrug. ● Member, Council of Nationalities Commission on Social and Economic Development of Union and Autonomous Republics, and Autonomous Oblasts and Okrugs.

From the Ust-Ordynsky Buryat Autonomous Okrug (RSFSR)

Batorov, Oleg Borisovich
● Second secretary, Osinsky Raikom, Irkutsk Oblast, RSFSR. CPSU member. Elected from NTO No. 746, Ust-Ordynsky Buryat Autonomous Okrug. ● Member, SupSov Committee on *Glasnost*, Rights, and Appeals of Citizens.

From the Yamalo-Nenets Autonomous Okrug (RSFSR)

Rugin, Roman Prokopevich
● Writer; senior teaching specialist at the House of Culture of the Peoples of the North, Salekhard. CPSU member. Elected from NTO No. 750, Yamalo-Nenets Autonomous Okrug. ● Member, Council of Nationalities Commission on Culture, Language, National and Interethnic Traditions, and Preservation of Historical Heritage.

Index of Delegates

163

FORTHCOMING BOOKS FROM RADIO LIBERTY

The USSR in 1989: A Record of Events

Compiled by Vera Tolz; edited by Melanie Newton . . . . . A year's collection of "The USSR This Week," the highly acclaimed feature of Radio Liberty's weekly *Report on the USSR, The USSR in 1989: A Record of Events* is the first in an annual series that will create a cumulative historical record of what is happening in the USSR, consolidate it in a single volume, and make it—plus source references—conveniently accessible in a lasting form. *early 1990*

A Biographic Directory of 100 Leading Soviet Officials

Compiled by Alexander Rahr . . . . . The latest (fifth) edition of the directory published since 1981 contains details about the careers of current members of the top Soviet Party and government bodies, officials of the armed forces and diplomats, as well as other officials who are believed to have a good chance of attaining top-level posts in the next few years. Major changes from earlier editions including photographs of the Soviet officials. *late 1989*

A Biographic Directory of Soviet Regional Party Leaders

Compiled by Gavin Helf . . . . . An important element in making and implementing policy, Soviet regional Party leaders also serve as a constant pool of new talent for promotion to the center. Intended to fill gaps in our knowledge of the careers and affiliations of the new generation of leaders promoted under Andropov, Chernenko, and Gorbachev, this third edition of the directory was compiled at the same time as the *Biographic Directory of 100 Leading Soviet Officials*, so there is no overlap. Rather, the two volumes complement one another. Photographs included. *late 1989*

Perestroika & the Private Sector of the Soviet Economy
Proceedings of a Radio Liberty Conference, Munich, July 7 and 8, 1989

Edited by John Tedstrom . . . . . Contents: **Robert Campbell**—How to Think about *Perestroika;* **Elizabeth Teague**—Redefining Socialism in the USSR; **Mark von Hagen**—NEP, *Perestroika,* and the Problem of Alternatives; **Philip Hanson**—Ownership Issues under *Perestroika;* **Vlad Sobell**—Lessons from Eastern Europe; **John Tedstrom**—The Reemergence of Soviet Cooperatives; **Theodor Schweisfurth**—Legal Aspects of Soviet Economic Reform; **Karl-Eugen Wädekin**—Is There a Privatization of Soviet Agriculture?; **Hans Heymann, Jr.**—*Perestroika* and Innovation in Soviet Industry; **Perry L. Patterson**—Are There Commodity and Financial Markets in the Soviet Future?; **Michael Alexeev**—Retail Price Reform in the Soviet Union; **Aaron Trehub**—*Perestroika* and Social Entitlements. *late 1989*

Radio Liberty, 1775 Broadway, New York, NY 10019, (212) 397-5300
Radio Liberty, Oettingenstraße 67, D-8000 München, FRG, (049-089) 2102-3320

Other CSISBOOKS of Related Interest

Gorbachev's Military Policy in the Third World

Mark N. Katz . . . . . Useful background on postwar Soviet policy; detailed analysis of how Gorbachev's administration has and has not moved away from earlier precedents. Author argues that Gorbachev seeks to reduce Soviet exposure in the Third World while continuing to maintain Soviet positions in selected states, particularly those of strategic value to the USSR.

CSIS The Washington Paper $32.95 hc $11.95 pb   1989

Paradoxes of Soviet Reform: The Nineteenth Communist Party Conference

Dawn Mann . . . . . "Dawn Mann is already well known as one of the brightest representatives of the new generation of American Sovietologists. She confirms this reputation with the present essay, one of the best published analyses about the main event of the tumultuous year 1988 in the Soviet Union."—from the foreword by Michel Tatu.

Significant Issues Series $8.95   1988

Coping with Gorbachev's Soviet Union

Stephen Sestanovich, Andrew C. Goldberg, Francis Fukuyama, and Bruce D. Porter What should the United States want in the medium to long-term relationship with the Soviet Union? This monograph examines the economic and political steps that are most conducive to the achievement of U.S. goals and building a strong U.S.-Soviet relationship.

Significant Issues Series $6.95   1988

Gorbachev's Information Revolution: Controlling Glasnost in a New Electronic Era

Wilson P. Dizard and S. Blake Swensrud . . . . . The Soviet government sharply increased funding for telecommunications and information facilities after the 27th Party Congress in 1986. The authors believe the efforts can improve Soviet economic performance.

Significant Issues Series/Westview $21.50   1987

Purchase in the CSIS Bookroom at 1800 K Street, NW, Suite 718, Washington, DC 20006 or order by telephone (202-775-3119). Prepay with VISA or MasterCard or check. Please make checks out to CSISBOOKS. Add $1.75 for postage and handling.

All books listed under **Selected Titles** (inside back cover) are $6.95.

☐ VISA ☐ MASTERCARD _____ Expiration Date

Name _____

Account No. _____ Telephone No. _____

Ship to _____

_____

_____

From CSIS Bookroom 1800 K Street, N.W. Suite 400 Washington, D.C. 20006